September 1, 2004
To Ted, who can make Cape
days turn golden in time
for weddings!
With best wishes,
Al

8-31-04
Wedding of Stephen Lipes
+ Cathy Herbst.
At Forestead PA Beach.

Golden Days

Memories of a Golden Retriever

ARTHUR VANDERBILT

Willow Creek
P R E S S

© 1998 Arthur T. Vanderbilt

Illustrations © 2002 William Ersland

Published by Willow Creek Press
P.O. Box 147, Minocqua, Wisconsin 54548

For information on other Willow Creek Press titles, call 1-800-850-9453

ISBN 1-57223-581-0 Willow Creek Press 2002
First published by Bantam Books in 1998.

Library of Congress Cataloging-in-Publication Data
Vanderbilt, Arthur
Golden days : memories of a golden retriever / Arthur Vanderbilt
p.   cm.
ISBN 0553-11083-7 (original edition)
1. Golden retriever—Massachussets—Cape Cod—Anecdotes.
2. Dogs—Massachussets—Cape Cod—Anecdotes.
3. Vanderbilt, Arthur.   I Title
SF429.G63V35   1998
818'.5403—dc21   97-32215
CIP

Printed in Canada

Golden Days

"To his dog, every man is Napoleon"
—ALDOUS HUXLEY

"I would like, to begin with, to say that though parents, husbands, children, lovers and friends are all very well, they are not dogs."
—ELIZABETH VON ARNIM

Chapter One

A Morning in October

What is it about golden retrievers that can break your heart?

Is it their love unconditional, love unqualified, love in its purest form?

The range of their emotions, from unimaginable joy to unthinkable sorrow?

Their original peculiarities that form unforgettable personalities?

Their inexhaustible enthusiasm that keeps familiar routines from ever becoming boring?

Is it the mischievous gleam in their eye that precedes the unexpected?

Is it their seemingly uncanny insight into our lives? The worries and concerns and wisdom you can read so well in their expressions as they mull things over?

"All knowledge," Kafka wrote, "the totality of all questions and answers, is contained in the dog."

Is it their beguiling seductiveness as they nuzzle you and lean into you and smack a wet sloppy kiss on you and give bare legs and arms a leisurely tongue bath and lay their heads on your lap to doze off?

What is it, I wondered that Saturday morning last October, as I lay in the sunlight on the carpet in the front hall of my parents' house, saying goodbye to Amy, their golden retriever, who had had a crush on me for the last ten years.

No one could say it yet, but Amy, we knew, was dying.

She lived with my parents. They had retired to Cape Cod, the three of them, but hadn't yet sold their house in New Jersey and had returned here for a high school reunion. Amy had been fine when they drove down from the Cape a week before. And she had certainly been fine when I stopped at their house Wednesday evening to visit with the friends who had come over for dessert.

As always, when I pull up in front of the house she is there waiting at the front screen door, barking wildly when she sees me get out of the car, pawing desperately at the door until it's opened. And when it is, she bursts out, full speed. I step off the front walk onto the lawn to better brace myself for what's coming: an eighty-seven-pound retriever linebacker hurtling toward me. She leaps up, wrapping her front paws around me, squeezing tightly.

"Get inside before the neighbors see," my parents had always called out under their breath, but not this evening. After watching this spectacle for all these years, they have come to accept that, for whatever reason, I am Amy's Tom Cruise, her Brad Pitt, her Elvis.

"What a gracious hostess," I say, patting her as she squeals in delight and at last drops down with a sigh, happily herding me into the house. Tail wagging proudly at what she has brought home, she heads straight to the front hall closet, dancing circles in front of it, barking at it, looking at me to hurry up and stop all the idle chatter.

"Is there something in there for Amy?" I innocently ask, playing my role to perfection, just as she likes it.

Rumbling growls of eagerness as she paws to get the door open.

Ever so cautiously, I open the closet door. She pushes her way in through the opening crack, rummaging with abandon through a jumble of winter boots and rubbers, an assortment of miscellaneous umbrellas, sneakers, and walking shoes until she locates in the dusty clutter exactly what she's after: one of my old fleece-lined slippers. She grabs hold of it, emerges from the closet, tosses her head back in triumph, and races into the dining room and around the dining room table with me in hot pursuit.

"Out of the way! Get out of the way!" my father reminds my mother, knowing by heart all the rules of the shoe game and that this routine will have to play itself out — before our guests arrive, we hope.

"I get you!" I shout at Amy, chasing her in dizzying circles around the table. "I get you!"

Round and around we go until she lets me catch up to her. I sit down in front of her, each holding an end of the slipper as we stare into each other's eyes.

"Why, Amy, thank you. Thank you so very much! This, you know, is my favorite slipper, my very best slipper."

Actually, from years of playing this mysterious retriever game, the slipper is getting pretty ratty.

"Can I have it to keep my foot nice and warm? Please? Pretty please?"

She relaxes her hold on the moist slipper just enough for me to extricate it.

"Thank you, Amy. Thank you." We touch noses, and I rub my face into the warm wonderful dog smell of her shoulder. She licks my ear. "That was so kind of you to fetch my shoe like a real retriever. Good girl!"

She watches closely as I return the slipper to the hall closet so that it's ready for my next visit.

But she starts limping the next morning and spends the rest of that day lying on the loveseat in the den. A hobbling limp that doesn't get any better. No interest in eating; not a good sign. My parents take her to the vet. Something stuck in her paw? Lyme disease? She's had that before. Arthritis? She is getting older. Dr. Walters takes an x-ray of her leg and the overlap of the shot shows the lymphoma in her chest.

Animals, scientists tell us, can fake good health when they are very sick to such an extent that naturalists have watched birds singing on a tree limb until the moment they fall to the ground, dead. My guess is that Amy has been faking it for quite a while to keep up her routines to please us, but now no longer can.

Saturday morning. My parents are off running errands. They'll be driving back to the Cape tomorrow morning after the reunion. I stop by their house to visit Amy, hoping to find her feeling better and that maybe I can get her to eat; knowing I am saying goodbye.

I let myself in through the garage and creep up the stairs to see if I can surprise her.

There she is, stretched out in the front hall, her head under the chair by the telephone table, sound asleep.

"Amy? Amy?"

She turns her head just an inch or two to make eye contact, thumps her tail weakly, and closes her eyes again. No special retriever hug this morning. I pretend nothing's different.

"How are you? How's Amy?" I ask her, lying down right next to her and patting her silky smooth head. "Amy okay?"

The heat is coming up in the radiators. After a while, I open the front door to let in the fresh air. It's one of those beautiful, blue sky, green grass football mornings of early autumn when Death whispers in the rustle of the brown oak leaves falling, settling on the lawn, "Live: I'm coming."

Her eyes open. The sun is warm on her back. Her nose twitches, smelling the wet grass and dying leaves.

"It's nice out there, isn't it?" I want to bring her some good news. "Hey, you know you're going to the Cape tomorrow, right? Jean, Bill, and, Amy. That's right. Tomorrow!"

She closes her eyes but her nose keeps twitching, inhaling all the scents of her tenth autumn. And as we lie together in the sunlight in the front hall that Saturday morning in October, the breeze in the hemlocks begins to sound like the surf along the Cape's outer shore, and I'm sure we're thinking the same thoughts, remembering the same golden days . . . .

Chapter Two

Homecomings

*I*t's July. The first weekend in July. The time, 11:30 a.m. The last leg of a long trip on a hot summer Saturday morning. My sister has flown in from Washington, D.C. I arrive from Newark. We meet downstairs at the baggage area of the Delta terminal, take the bus around and around Logan to the Hertz lot, find our car, throw our bags in the back seat, and join the weekend traffic heading out to the Cape. The noonday heat rises off the highway ahead of us, forming mirage puddles that evaporate as we reach them. The traffic is moving along. Then it slows for no reason. Now, inexplicably, it stops. We don't move twenty feet in fifteen minutes. It starts up again unexpectedly.

And, of course, when we finally see the Sagamore Bridge we're moving stop and start, bumper to bumper. Crossing the Cape Cod Canal, we shut off the air-conditioner and open the windows to inhale the scent of scrub pine and saltwater that to us signifies the beginning of summer. We count off the exits along the Mid-Cape Highway that appear and disappear in tedious slow motion. Finally, at Exit 11, we pull off and continue along Bay Road, noting the new construction since Thanksgiving and then, ahead of us, the expanse of Pleasant Bay, with wind surfers darting across the water and, farther out, white sails slipping by the islands.

As we drive by the golf course, past panoramic views out over the Bay and islands all the way to the outerbeach, we unbuckle our seat belts, getting ready to get out of the car the second we roll into the driveway and come to a stop. For we know that there, looking out through the front screen door, will be a golden retriever who will instantly know that the two missing members of her pack are home.

She's up on her hind legs, pawing and pawing at

the screen, barking frantically. Heeding her alert, another pack member opens the screen door and out she explodes, jumping onto us, snuggling her face against us, squeezing tight in delight, from one to the other, then racing in circles around us, with happy squealings and squeakings, a bark of joy right in the face as we kneel down to say hello, and then we're shepherded into the house straight to our bedrooms.

We place our suitcases on the floor and unzip them as Amy pokes her nose in mine, shuffling through the neat stacks of underwear and socks, pushing aside the shirts, searching.

"What do you want, Amy? Where is it? This? Oh, here it is!"

I dig in to the exact spot and pull out the new tennis ball with the delicious rubbery smell. She snatches it and races out of the room, tearing around the house with the ball in her mouth, whining and whimpering, blowing out through her nose in excitement, looking, looking, trying to locate the perfect hiding spot.

Behind the curtain? No, too obvious.

Under the chair? No good, they're all watching.

What to do? She lies down and gets in a few good chews, then at once is up again, ball in mouth, trotting over to lead us outside along the sandy path down the bluff to the beach to survey her domain.

She stops at the end of the path so that we can take it all in. The southwest breeze blowing through the beach grass. Summer smells of hot sand and cool saltwater and of the green salt marsh over on Strong Island. Down the Bay, Little Sipson and Big Sipson islands, and behind them in Little Bay, Hog Island, Sampson Island, Pochet Island, and Barley Neck. Beyond, the rolling dunes of the outerbeach. Above, the summer sky.

A dash to the water's edge. A look back at us: *Do you want to go swimming? No? Not now? Okay.* Back up to the house she races, checking to make sure we're right behind her. Straight to the kitchen to her water dish. She drinks and drinks, then rushes to join us in the sunroom, sitting down in the middle of the room and breathing an immense sigh of contentment.

Then and only then can we say hello to our parents.

"You know, she's been waiting patiently by the door all morning."

We get caught up on the news. Amy observes the conversation, her eyes moving from speaker to speaker, until all the really interesting gossip has been told and the talk gets boring and repetitive, at which point she lies down, her paws casually crossed, and closes her eyes. Every now and then she looks over to make sure we're still there, makes eye contact and thumps her tail up and down against the floor: *One*, bang! *Two*, bang! *Three*, bang! *Four*, bang! *Oh yes, they're all here.*

For the rest of the afternoon, she follows us around, stealing glances at us with that they're-really-actually-finally-here look. At dinner, she assumes her usual place, seated right between my sister and me with her head resting first on my sister's lap, then on mine, then back again, every once in a while smacking her nose into our stomachs to make sure her secret code still works. It does; against all parental edicts, after each smack a tasty morsel of flounder or clump of macaroni and cheese mysteriously finds its way from our plates into her mouth; and later, for dessert, a container of yogurt (lemon is our favorite) is shared, pretty much fifty-fifty. (When no one is looking, we together eat carrot strips, one starting at one end, the other at the other.)

And in the middle of the night in my dreams I hear a soft swishing and feel a presence, and opening one eye, see her head resting on the mattress a few inches from my face, staring at me. Seeing me open an eye, she swats her tail back and forth into the bed in greeting, her body wiggling in happiness.

"Hello, Amy," I say softly, patting her. Satisfied that I'm okay, she's immediately on her way to the next bedroom for a bed check, coming back once or twice more during the night to make sure, really sure, we're still there.

The first summer, when she was just a pup, when she had first checked on me in the night, I assumed she had to go outside.

"Amy want to go out?" I had whispered.

She looked at me, quizzically. *What the heck is his problem?*

"Amy? Okay, Amy go out?"

Well, okay, if he has to, but this is really weird.

It's pitch black and scary out there and morning has got to be a long way off and I've got to make my rounds and get back to bed.

We'd creep through the house with a flashlight, out the side door, crossing the patio and the wet grass to the top of the bluff.

The Bay was making its liquid sounds. Far off, we could hear the surf breaking up and down the outerbeach and sometimes the hollow crash of an immense breaker. Starlight that had started toward us a million years before reached us at last that night. Looking out from the bluff at the Milky Way extending horizon to horizon, filling the vast night sky, it felt as if we were alone together in inter-planetary space, as if the earth was moving in space and time, an island adrift in a sea of stars, and that if we didn't hold on, we could fall off.

"Here. Amy go here," I'd say, pointing the flashlight's beam on a nice spot in the poverty grass on the crest of the bluff.

What the. . .?

"Okay, here. Amy. Amy go here."

No dice. She stares at me.

"Okay, but I'm telling you, this is your last

chance, okay? I'm not coming out here again, okay? You understand that, right? This is it."

No.

"No?"

No.

"Okay. Last chance. Here, okay?" I say, flashing the light around the grass. "Amy go here."

No.

"No?"

No.

By then, we had both scared ourselves with thoughts of what might be lurking at that time of night out in the dark behind the bayberry thickets: coyotes? bears? drug-runners? kidnappers? I scooped Amy up onto my shoulder and hurried back to the house, locking the door behind us.

We both go back to bed. Several hours later I again feel the presence, the swish of a tail, the eager eyes.

"See Amy? I told you. You have to go out. And this time, you're going to do something, okay?

And out we'd go and back we'd come, no farther ahead.

After several nights of this, a glimmer of slow-witted human comprehension: Amy didn't want to go outside. In fact, she has extraordinary bladder control. Rather, she was making her nightly bed checks.

Several times a night, from bedroom to bedroom she goes on her rounds to make sure everyone is all right. As long as we say hello or give her a pat, off she goes, satisfied that all is well. But if we're sleeping soundly, out like a log, she'll make her soft whining noises or bat her tail against the bed or rest her head on the mattress, staring at us until we awaken. If, perchance, a bedroom door is closed and her little noises fail to draw a response, she'll stand next to the door and wag her tail so that on each sweep it slams against the door. And if we're really out cold and that too fails to do the trick, she'll lie down outside the door, stretched right against it; and just like Atticus Finch watching over Jem at the end of *To Kill a Mockingbird*, she'll be there all night, and she'll be there when we open our doors in the morning, thumping her tail and making her morning sounds of greeting.

Up from her bed in my parents' bedroom, out into the hall, through the dark living room and kitchen she makes her way each night for her nightly head counts, down the back hall to my sister's bedroom. A quick check. Into my room. All is well. Everyone is in. All present and accounted for. Everything is as it should be. And so, back to her bed and to sleep.

Like a card counter in a casino, she always, constantly, in the back of her mind is counting who is there and who is missing; and if the numbers don't add up to four, she senses that something is wrong and worries. She's like Nana, the nursery watchdog in *Peter Pan* who tended the Darling children, Wendy, John, and Michael. Watching over us is pretty much a full-time job for Amy, what with the vigils at the front door, the bed checks, the worrying.

She's considered herself in charge right from the afternoon my parents picked her up to bring home. Breeders recommend weeks twelve to sixteen as the best time to take a puppy home for the easiest transition. Due to travel circumstances, Amy was only eight weeks old when she began living with my parents. Either she assumed from the outset that she is human, or they did a pretty good imitation of being golden retrievers; they did know how to pass themselves off as such. From the moment she swaggered into their house, like Caesar on a triumphal march surveying his latest conquest (although, unlike Caesar, her bravery always seems like someone whistling in the dark; and if something is a little frightening, she'll beat a hasty retreat to the safety of the nearest legs), she assumed her rightful position as pack leader.

It's a ragtag pack if ever there was one: a retired couple and two middle-aged children who come for visits (usually only when the Cape's weather is good), but she makes the most of what she has. The same dog who opens presents with all the enthusiasm of a four-year-old seems to sense with a philosopher's wisdom that "Old Time is still a-flying"; she considers the return of any pack member who has been away from the house for an hour or more grounds for an effusive reunion; a return after a more lengthy absence warrants a full-blown homecoming celebration.

Chapter Three

Pack Maneuvers

The summer heat and humidity hangs around day after day, for four days and five, forever. Sometime during the night, the wind shifts and blows in through the screen and you pull up the sheet and the light blanket, squished at the bottom of the bed, and later hear the wind waves piling up along the beach below the bluff and smell the freshness of the summer morning.

On a morning like this, even the sleepyheads (and Amy can be the queen of the sleepyheads, waiting for the last pack member to get up and dressed before she decides to arise, but who can blame her? She's been on duty all night, watching over her flock), even the sleepyheads are up early today. The sun is so dazzling bright, the sky so infinitely blue, that from the breakfast table you can see all the way up the Bay to Pochet Island and beyond, between the dunes of the outerbeach, deep blue glimpses of the sea.

It feels like the first morning, this morning of the good sailing breeze blowing through the beach grass at the edge of the lawn and the branches of the apple tree outside the open dining room window, billowing out the curtains; a morning to inhale, to drink in, to absorb. Amy, who has already been out and had breakfast, feels it too. She is especially impatient for adventure to begin and plots ways to hurry us along.

She appears, after a suspicious absence, with a stray Top-Sider and, once she is sure we've noticed, shakes it vigorously back and forth, growling. She looks up at us and shakes it again.

I glance at it. It looks like Marjorie's, so, unconcerned, I go back to my bowl of Shredded Wheat.

"That's yours, you know," my sister informs me quite a few minutes later as she munches contentedly on a jelly doughnut and as Amy samples the rawhide laces of the Topsider, getting them nice and mushy.

I look again. I spring from the table.

"That's mine! I get you!" I shout, shaking my fist at the thief as she races around and around the table with me almost, but never quite, able to grab hold of the end of a bushy tail circling in happiness.

Speed won't do the trick. After all, her ancestors were able to run down herds of wildebeests on the savannas of Africa; and outside on the lawn, not even two of us stand a chance when she plays keep-away, with her cunning twists and turns and brazen dashes between us. Time to apply man's superior intelligence.

I feint and turn and head straight at her as she loops around the table. Without missing a beat, she slips under the table, squiggling through the forest of chair legs and out the other side, now behind me. I try the maneuver again, changing directions. Same result.

Damn! I'm not about to be outwitted by a smart-ass golden retriever. If I could just take a minute to think about it, I'm sure I could plot some strategy to corner her. I'm sure I could. But with a stomach filled with a tumbler of Tropicana, half a bowl of bite-sized Shredded Wheat topped with sliced banana, part of a jelly doughnut, and a glass of milk, I'm ready to wave the white flag of surrender.

I sit down on the floor.

"That's my favorite Top-Sider, you know."

She stops on the other side of the table. No response. She'll take no prisoners.

I pick up her green rubber frog and begin negotiating.

"Would Amy like froggie? Would she? Would Amy like froggie?

I hold it up and squeak it a couple times.

Not even looking at froggie, Amy makes a great show of busily chewing my shoe.

"She's not going to give you *your* shoe for *her* frog," my sister explains to me as if talking to a simpleton. "You've got to give her a piece of nana."

"No," my mother commands. "She's had enough banana. You've both spoiled her, and this is what happens. She never does this when Bill and I are alone, do you, Amy?"

From Amy's expression, I have serious doubts about that. Or maybe Amy just considers us the easiest of her pack members to bully.

"You know why I need my shoe, don't you?" I say, now trying reasoning since negotiations have broken down. "So my foot won't get cold."

She looks at me, not about to fall for the soothing sweet talk of the vanquished.

"See? My foot doesn't have those nice pads like yours."

I hold up my bare foot and run my finger along the sole so she can see the difference.

"How can I even go for a walk without it? I don't know what to do now," I sadly sigh. "Now I can't even go for a walk."

Walk is probably the word that does it. She comes over cautiously, suspiciously, holding the Top-Sider by the laces and letting it bob back and forth like a trophy as she walks. She sits down facing me.

"Thank you, Amy," I say as I pry open her jaws to extract the soggy shoe.

"That is so gross," my sister grimaces. "Yeech. Dog slobber. Get it out of here."

"Thank you so much, Amy," I say again, hugging her.

I get up and place the Top-Sider out of reach on top of the dryer in the kitchen and sit down to continue eating my cereal.

This, clearly, is not at all what Amy is trying to communicate; and she looks at us with disgust — *They really are dense* — before stalking out to the kitchen. Within a minute she returns, this time with the hand towel from the back of the kitchen door, which she flips back and forth over her head, challenging us.

"Someone get that," my mother orders.

"I'm not getting it this time," I announce, huddling over my breakfast.

"Okay, okay," Marjorie grumbles, taking off after her through the same familiar routine.

And so, like a sheep dog, she keeps herding her simple flock in the direction she has chosen; and much sooner than without her prodding, she is nudging us out the patio door, outside into the beautiful morning, and we're following her down the bluff along the sandy path to the beach.

We zip up our windbreakers. The fresh northwest breeze, which is coming straight down the Bay from the Narrows, has overnight rolled up a glistening green eelgrass bulwark along the tide line and is splashing the waves in a jumble up against it.

Amy dashes ahead down the beach, turning to us and then scooting back straight to the fingers of the one holding her tennis ball, which fingers she tries to gobble, then goes out long like an outfielder, looking back over her shoulder as she runs.

"Throw it!" we shout.

My father throws the ball in a high pop; and Amy, racing at top speed, is right there as it comes down. She snags it and runs on down the beach into the wind, tail wagging, ears blowing back, charging the breeze in sheer delight as if it were something to play with, with us behind her, jogging a middle-aged golden-years jog along the sand just above where the small waves are tumbling over each other.

Way ahead of us, Amy stops, drops her ball, and looks out over the Bay. Like a connoisseur sampling a fine wine, she raises her head into the wind, sniffs with curiosity to identify the vintage, sniffs again with mounting conviction and pleasure, closes her eyes and sniffs some more, because the air is so smooth with its captivating bouquet of the Bay. Satisfied, on she goes, gamboling along down the beach ahead of us, scouting the terrain. She dramatically charges a flock of sandpipers; plays tag with the waves; then falls back behind us, tracking a scent in the beach grass.

This is more like it, she undoubtedly is thinking as we noisily troop along. *I've finally gotten my pathetic excuse for a pack out on a hunt.*

On a morning like this, when the wind shifts to the northwest and the weather clears, our moods change. There is a feeling that something is happening. Shadows of clouds sprint over the water. Ahead of us, off the dock at the town landing, the three sailboats buck and bounce at their moorings, the waves pushing under their gleaming white hulls, their halyards pinging against the metal masts.

Waves splash up the beach, one on top of the other, and the wind moves through the patch of marsh grass along the water's edge and whiffles under our windbreakers and turns Amy's ears inside out and sighs through the silver-green beach grass back in the dunes.

> *And all I ask is a windy day with the white*
> *   clouds flying*
> *And the flung spray and blown spume, and the*
> *   seagulls crying.*

We duck under the dock, which Amy seems to regard as delineating the far boundary of her domain—it's the last point along the beach from which home is visible. No matter how many times we've walked this beach, as always, she emerges from the dock's dark shadow with all the anticipation and wonder of a child entering Disneyland. Ahead lies the frontier, the wilderness, adventure.

Here, past the town landing, a forest of scraggly poplars and scrub pine comes right down to the sand below the golf course. Amy pokes around the winter wrack line, sniffing in the jumble of bittersweet and salt spray rose, as we look for perfect scallop shells in lustrous shades of pink and yellow and deep mahogany and search for lucky stones, those gray, wave-smoothed pebbles with a white line mysteriously circling them.

"Here, look at this," my mother says, pointing to a waterlogged strip of wood flush in the sand that the tides have uncovered. It extends down the beach and out into the water.

"From the old hotel," my father says, digging around it with a shell. "Part of the pier."

"Where was it? Up there?" my mother asks, pointing to where the green of the golf course sweeps down a hill all the way to the shore.

"I think it was right over there, on the fourth fairway, with that view out over the Bay."

We debate once again where it was sited, armed now with this new clue the Bay has revealed, this strip of wood from the old pier, all that remains of a grand turn-of-the-century hotel, the Hotel Chatham.

A few years ago we found in a bookstore in town a yellowed brochure put out by the hotel in its second year of operation, 1891. Two trains a day were available to bring guests from the Old Colony Station in Boston to the end of the line in Chatham (near today's municipal airport). From there the guests were taken by horse-drawn carriage the six or seven miles to the hotel. "The roadways are in fair condition," the brochure charitably noted; "Many tons of seashells are used annually on the roads . . . nothing contributes so much to the pleasure of a drive as a good shell road."

If it takes us two hours to drive from Boston to Chatham, assuming no heavy back-ups at the Bridge, the trip on June 28, 1890, the hotel's opening day, no doubt was a long day's journey, the last several miles of which, over those good shell roads, may have been somewhat less pleasurable to the weary travellers than the brochure promised.

Built by Marcellous Eldredge, Chatham's first millionaire, and Eben Jordan, the co-founder of Boston's Jordan Marsh department store, the Hotel Chatham was a huge three-story shingled structure with gambrel and tower roof, an ambitious edifice set out here in the middle of nowhere in a town with a population then of maybe a thousand. The floor plans showed thirty-five guest rooms on the second floor, with one "Gents" room containing one tub and two "arsenals" and one "Ladies" room with two tubs and five "arsenals." On the third floor, with its thirty-eight guest rooms, the one Gents room had two "arsenals" and the Ladies room five, with no tubs for either, an arrangement that strikes me, who shares one bathroom with one sister, as doomed from the outset. The "Grand Piazza" on the bayside was large enough to accommodate all "loiterers and promenaders," and inside there was a billiards room dedicated to "men who like to enjoy the selfish pleasure of their kind without intrusion."

To entertain those guests who happened not to be into loitering, promenading, or enjoying selfish pleasure, there were a host of other activities: "a long line of bath houses," seven miles of beaches owned by the hotel (which was either a typo in the brochure or an extraordinary statement about the low cost of this prime waterfront real estate in 1890), boating, fishing, clamming, tennis, croquet, indoor bowling, archery, trap shooting, fowl and fox hunting, and riding stables and trails.

The hotel never made a go of it (undoubtedly the bathroom arrangement had something to do with that). By the financial panic of 1907, it was bankrupt, its contents auctioned off. Before it was demolished when the golf course was built in the early 1920s, the huge boarded-up and abandoned structure was a favorite spot for picnickers and players of hide-and-seek.

It always seems that something more of the old hotel could be uncovered if we poked around in the woods above the beach: the outlines of the tennis court at least, or remnants of trails, a long lost croquet ball, something.

"I bet we could probably find some old pieces of china back in there," someone suggests, but thoughts of poison ivy and ticks come to mind and anyhow, the pack is on the move again.

A pair of goldfinches dart out of the woods ahead of us and roller coaster over to the small orange flowers of the milkweed and the red berries and purple thistles heads where once the bathhouses stood. Any shades of nineteenth-century promenaders and loiterers must have been off fox hunting, for it feels this morning like we're the first walkers of this beach since the beginning of time; and the sight of another's footprints in the sand would have been, as it was for Robinson Crusoe, a momentous occasion.

Actually, we're far from the first, millennia from the first.

Late on one of those gray afternoons when fog closes in over the outerbeach, drifting down the Bay so that it's hard to tell where beach ends and water begins, then sometimes we can walk these shores and sense the others.

Archaeologists working around the Bay have seen them in fragments of stone implements, shell deposits, traces of ancient campfire sites, bits and pieces of evidence in which they have been able to watch the Native Americans wandering these shores ten thousand years ago, at the end of the Pleistocene Epoch, a few thousand years after the retreat of the last glaciers.

Ten thousand years ago. It was only five hundred years ago that Columbus reached the New World. One thousand years ago that the Norsemen were raiding European settlements. Two thousand years ago that Christ was walking the shores of Galilee. Three thousand years ago that Troy fell on the shores of the Aegean. Over four thousand years ago that Pharaoh Cheops ordered the construction of the Great Pyramid by the Nile. Recorded history gets pretty murky much beyond that, yet it was another six thousand years before the Great Pyramid arose that early people haunted these shores, right where we're walking this morning.

Who were they? Where did they come from? How did they find this outer shore? Everything these nomadic food gatherers needed was here: a shallow bay of hidden harbors and coves, with estuaries and salt marshes full of fish and shellfish, visited by waterfowl and birds, the fields a tangle of growth with wild grains and fruits. There were freshwater ponds and springs, and forests filled with game. Big game at that. Surprisingly, bear, moose, and wolf bones dating back to prehistoric times have been dug up around these quiet waters. Wolves, Amy! Maybe you're following in the footsteps of a much-distant relative. A stash of corn recently uncovered near Ryder's Cove radiocarbon dated back to 1100—the depths of the Dark Ages in Europe—giving evidence that these people by then had begun planting crops and living a more settled existence around the Bay.

Amy is nosing around the dried mats of eelgrass that cover the upper beach, sprinting down to the edge of the Bay, wading into the forest green water still shaded from the morning sun by the high bluff, looking at us to see if we might consider joining her for a morning dip, racing back up the beach to poke around in the beach grass and scrub growth of briers and grasses. Has she picked up a trace of Mr. Fox exploring the beach last night for a snack, or can she sense the presence of some of these ancient Bay people? If archaeologists can read in tiny bits of chipped stone the story of an ancient people, could the incredibly sensitive nose of a dog pick up the presence of people and animals past?

Maybe. Maybe her earnest sniffing is giving her more clues than the archaeologists can read in their fragments. Who knows? But this is certain: that on a July morning, ten thousand years ago, on a morning just like this when a fresh northwest breeze was blowing down the Bay from the islands, some of these people were looking out over the sun-dazzled water and, just like us, drawing a deep breath.

Up ahead, for the sport of it, a gull is banking off the wind, soaring down along the beach, calling and crying and laughing as if it has a message for us. (*Live! Live,* it would be telling us, if we had been listening.) As effortlessly as a child's kite, it rides an updraft over the high bluff of Great Point, up into that blue summer sky.

From the top of Great Point, the highest spot around the Bay, did Indian scouts spot the tiny *Mayflower* struggling off the outerbeach that November morning in 1620 before it escaped from the "dangerous shoals and roaring breakers" and headed back north to Plymouth? And years before that, the ship of Captain John Smith in 1614 as he sailed along the outerbeach, drawing the first accurate map of the coast? Or Henry Hudson in 1609, sailing south toward New York? Or Bartholomew Gosnold in 1602, whose fascination with the schools of cod gave the peninsula its name? Or Giovanni da Verrazano in 1524 sailing north to

Maine, or the Cabots in 1498 passing these shores on their voyage from Labrador to Virginia? Or, for that matter, Leif Ericson in 1003 A.D. in his square-sailed longship gliding by the fifty miles of outerbeach, whose white sands, sparkling in the sun, may have been the Wonder Strand of the Norsemen?

The sandy face of this high bluff is layered with vertical knobby veins of dry gray clay. The clay, geologists tell us, was deposited during an intermission between the great ice ages, those aeons of days and nights of unimaginable chaos, of awesome desolation when glaciers melted and the sunless sea, which covered all of eastern Massachusetts, sorted and deposited in layers the materials the glaciers had been bulldozing forward. With a microscope, a geologist can identify in this clay the tiny fossils of sponges, shells, algae, and pollen which date back 15,000 years.

I break off a chunk and, as we walk along, roll it between my fingers, stopping to moisten it in the Bay, squeezing it out and shaping it as easily as with the best modeling clay from an art supply store. What bowls, in centuries past, were made of clay from this bluff? What marbles made in long-ago springs by boys walking this beach? I roll three marbles and leave them on top of the boulder at the base of the bluff, making a mental note to see if they're there, sunbaked, the next time.

Two Huck Finns in a Boston whaler with an oversized outboard zip by, skipping along right off the beach, bouncing up over the swells and slapping down with a roar. They wave at us as they pass, hitting the whitecaps at full speed and planing out of sight as they follow the shoreline around Great Point toward the head of the Bay.

They trace the exact route down the Bay some Pilgrims from Plymouth Plantation with their Indian guide, Squanto, sailed on a September morning three and a half centuries before on a voyage for survival.

The Pilgrim's first winter in the New World had been brutal. In January and February of 1621, half of their company died, many of typhus. Provisions were low. Shelters were not ready for winter. And these brave souls were surely questioning just what they had gotten themselves into. It was in these dark hours, their little settlement at Plymouth surrounded by a "hideous and desolate wilderness, full of wild beasts and wild men," that one of the wild men ventured forth toward them, speaking to them, incredibly, in broken English. Here was Squanto, who Governor Bradford later would describe as "a special instrument sent of God for their good, beyond their expectation."

A few years before, Squanto had been one of twenty-seven Indians captured by sailors from an English fishing vessel working the New England coastal waters and taken to Spain to be sold into slavery, probably as curiosities: the savages of the New World. Squanto managed to escape and make his way to England where he found employment with a merchant and learned English. Recognizing what an asset he could be as a guide and interpreter, the merchant took Squanto back to New England in 1618 on a trading mission. During an Indian attack on the English on Martha's Vineyard, he escaped again and made his way back to Plymouth.

In March of the Pilgrims' bleak winter of 1621, Squanto stepped out of that "hideous and desolate wilderness" and into history. It was he who told the Pilgrims about the alewives that would be running up the brooks in the spring and showed them how to trap them; it was he who taught them how to "fish the hills"—to use these fish as fertilizer, burying three beneath each mound they would plant with corn; it was he who served as their chief diplomat and barterer, assuring the surrounding Indian tribes that these strange people from another world were peaceful.

Even with Squanto's help, the Pilgrims' second year in the New World had been as difficult as the first. "Famine," Bradford wrote, was "beginning to pinch them severely." Provisions were exhausted. The *Mayflower* had returned to England, leaving them alone in the wilderness. Hoped-for supplies from England had not been forthcoming. It was daily more evident that the harvest was not going to be as bountiful as they had anticipated, with the settlers snatching corn even before it ripened. And though, as Bradford wrote, "many were well whipped when they were caught stealing a few ears of corn, hunger drove others to it, whom conscience did not restrain. It was quite clear that famine would prevail again next year if not prevented, or if their supplies, to which they dare not trust, should fail."

When English colonists in nearby Weymouth, suffering similar shortages, offered their sloop *Swan* for an expedition to seek supplies from neighboring Indian tribes, Governor Bradford in September 1622 organized an expeditionary force to the wilds of Cape Cod. Like the *Mayflower* before it, the *Swan* encountered those "dangerous shoals and roaring breakers" off the outerbeach and dared go no farther. Squanto piloted them over the outer bars and through the inlet, which at that time lay off Strong Island. "So they put into Manomoyick Bay," wrote Governor Bradford—Pleasant Bay—riding the current down the Bay to where the Monomoyick River emptied into the Bay (crossed today by Route 28), the site of the head village of the tribe of Monomoyicks.

No doubt the Monomoyick lookout atop Great Point's clay-veined bluff saw the *Swan* tossed in the whitewater off the outerbeach, followed its progress down the Bay and alerted the others, for when the sloop dropped anchor, all the Indians were hiding. Squanto went into the woods around the head of the Bay to persuade them that these white men were peaceful. Out they came, as one of the Pilgrims, Edward Winslow, described the scene, "welcoming our Governor according to their savage manner, refreshing them very well with store of venison and other victuals which they brought to them in great abundance."

It was here, right down the beach ahead of us, a little beyond the Chatham Yacht Club dock, that the Pilgrims bartered with the Indians for food. And here it was that Squanto died. As Governor Bradford wrote: "In this place Squanto fell sick of an Indian fever, bleeding much at the nose (which the Indians take as a symptom of death) and within a few days died there, desiring the Governor to pray for him that he might go to the Englishmen's God in Heaven; and bequeathed sundry of his things to sundry of his English friends as remembrances of his love; of which they had great loss."

This morning, the colorful sail of a catamaran skims with precision back and forth across the head of the Bay between Round Cove and the Wading Place, right where the *Swan* lay at anchor when Governor Bradford bartered for the twenty-eight hogsheads of corn and beans that would carry the Pilgrims through the winter. And up on the bluff overlooking the Bay, a golfer in lime green trousers and a pink Lecoste alligator shirt lines up his putt. When the golf course was under construction in 1921, excavations for bunker sixteen uncovered beneath a thicket of vines an Indian skeleton. It had not been buried in the usual Indian fashion but rather was found in a crude wooden coffin: Squanto?

From the underbrush at the base of the bluff emerges a bushy tail and rear end, pulling, tugging, an inch gained, two inches, the rustle of leaves, the snapping of twigs, a mighty tug and Amy appears, dragging a large branch, almost, but not quite, too big around for her mouth to grasp, and twice her size in length, with a network of smaller branches and a cluster of dead leaves clinging to one end, the whole encircled with wisps of dry eelgrass. Here, truly, is something worth the bartering!

At some point on every walk, she seems to pause and say to herself, *Hey, wait a minute: they still think I'm a retriever. I better find something good to bring home with me.* If she happens upon a choice discovery early on the walk, all to the good, she grabs it and proudly carries it all the way back with her. Sunbathers and swimmers who make the mistake of leaving their sandals or, Heaven forbid, their socks, neatly lined up by the side of their beach blankets, unattended, are certainly asking for trouble, especially if they aren't looking as Amy saunters by with her sweetest expression. Though an empty beer can is almost as good, as is a plank, an artistic piece of driftwood, a small log: treasures all. A real find is one of those rubber thong flip-flops (it makes no difference if it's a righty or lefty), and the rarest and most valuable discovery of all is a heavy rubber work glove a scalloper or quahoger has lost, especially if all the fingers are filled with sand and sticking out, followed in close second place by any glove at all, a surprising number of which she turns up on summer beaches. (It's something about gloves and socks. Fingers by themselves are not a problem; nor are toes. But fingers in gloves or toes in socks are beyond the pale, infuriating, maddening, and the offending glove or sock just has to be removed, yanked off, to reveal those curious hidden human appendages.)

Once Amy nosed around in the beach grass and came out with her mouth shut tight and a suspiciously innocent look in her eye. She has a habit of chewing (and sometimes when they are good and mushy, swallowing) all sorts of bad things—wads of aluminum foil she finds on the beach, tissues she steals from trash baskets, paper napkins snatched from where they fall under the dining room table, pine cones—things that aren't good for her, so spot inspections quite often are in order. On that particular summer's day we sat next to her and gently, slowly, pried open her jaws as she continued to pretend that there was absolutely nothing at all in there and—yes, this can be pretty gross—stuck a finger in, way back in the gizzard area, to see what she was hiding. Out came a wadded clump of paper which uncrumpled very nicely into three moist dollar bills. Lavish praise from one and all sent her back into the beach grass, returning in a remarkably short time with something else in closed mouth, the same look in her eye. Inspection time, and the magical slot machine spewed forth two more soggy dollars. Lyme tick haven or not, we charged into the beach grass to seek our fortune as Amy looked on, perversely refusing to assist us, obviously knowing then what it took four adults scrounging around on hands and knees in the sand a half hour to discover: there were only five one-dollar bills in that particular treasure cache.

If Amy has found nothing suitable by a certain point on a walk, she then begins an earnest search: a rather frantic foraging in the underbrush, testing the heft of stick after stick, but like Goldilocks, she is not easily satisfied. One stick is too puny for any self-respecting retriever; one, about the size of a small tree, is just too big to budge though she certainly gives it the old college try; none seem just right.

Now, being considerate pack members, we offer to lend a helping hand in assisting her search for the perfect stick. It should be, say, about two feet long, stripped of all bark, solid, clean, the perfect carrying stick. Right? Apparently not.

"Amy," we say, all excited, "here it is!" putting it next to her mouth, a stick any dog would be proud to carry.

Amy glances at it with unconcealed disdain, and as she turns her head away, we can almost hear her mutter to herself, *Well-meaning blatherskites!*

Though I would swear there are times when she forgets to add the "well-meaning" and just sneers "blatherskites!" or maybe something even stronger in dog language. Like all golden retrievers, Amy is affectionate and affable; but unlike many of her kind, she has moments when she does not always suffer fools gladly.

Clearly we know nothing about the proper selection of sticks. More and more frantically she pushes around in the dry undergrowth where winter storms and erosion of the bluff have deposited a messy storehouse of branches and limbs and driftwood, trying out one, then another, rejecting stick after stick, until finally, like now, she finds just what she's looking for, or at least a reasonable approximation thereof.

"Oh, Amy," my father says as she drags the branch away from the underbrush, "that's *much* too big. Drop it!"

She drops it, gets a better grip on it, and parades proudly down the beach, tail high, wisps of eelgrass blowing about it in the breeze, the leafy end rasping the sand as she goes, which seems to delight her all the more. The noisier the better. *Oh, I . . . love a parade!*

"Her poor jaw," my mother worries. "She can't carry that. Why does she do it?"

"It's too big for her," my father insists, hurrying to

catch up with her. "I'll break a piece off so it's at least manageable."

"I wouldn't do that if I were you," my sister advises, advice I would certainly have seconded had I not wanted to witness the bloody spectacle about to ensue. Just like watching the poor Christians thrown into the arena with the lions, as gory as you know it's going to get, you can't take your eyes off it.

The moment my father touches the end of the branch, and he does know enough not to go for the center, Amy drops it and lunges at the air, snarling and growling and baring her teeth, her hackles bristling. Here is a classic example of miscommunication between the species: my father knows he is helping; and Amy, projecting her dog values onto us, knows that anyone with a bit of sense would want to steal so carefully selected a stick.

"Okay, okay," my father says in disgust, strategically retreating, "see if I care."

"See, I told you," my sister says. "You can't take it away from her. That's hers. That's some kind of treasure."

"But she's going to hurt her jaw," my mother says. "You've got to get it away from her."

"Forget it," my sister wisely counsels.

So on down the beach we march, led by a proud retriever majorette carrying an enormous branch, precisely balanced, the branch see-sawing as she walks so that first one end scrapes the sand, then, as she readjusts, the other end. She couldn't drop it now even if she wants to, which she probably does after a few steps; now it's a matter of pride. She has fought off the surprise attack to steal her stick, and the prize is hers.

We're almost to the dock at the Chatham Yacht Club, our turn-around point. The float at the end of the long dock heaves and falls with the wind waves pushing down the Bay, groaning and complaining as it rubs against the two metal pilings that hold it in place. The flotilla of Bettlecats off the dock strain at their mooring lines where, a hundred years ago, twenty-five or thirty large catboats anchored, setting sail each morning before sunrise to head out the inlet to the Pollock Rip and Stone Horse Shoals for a day of cod fishing, returning with their catch, to the shanties that once lined this shore.

"Okay, Amy, turn around," my father says when we reach the dock.

Amy turns around to head back.

"Can't we go farther?" my sister objects. "This isn't far enough for her."

"Just up to the rocks," my father says in compromise.

Amy turns to continue on down the beach.

The tide is low, almost dead low, low dreen and about to turn, so the beach is wide. Just above the low tide line where I'm walking, with our pack leader strutting ahead of us on drier sand, a shallow depression in the sand, maybe a foot across, is filled with water that appears to be bubbling.

"Hey, look, I bet this is a spring," I call to the others, remembering reading about the springs that the Indians had used around this part of the Bay.

"That's not a spring," my sister says with contempt, walking over to look at it. "A spring wouldn't be in the water. That's going to be under water as soon as the tide comes in.

"That's right. That's what we feel when we hit the cold spots when we're swimming. Springs."

"No way."

I scoop out the sand in the depression. As I dig, the water comes to a full boil, bubbling up, ice cold, freezing cold, numbing cold water. The sand feathers out in the boiling ice water and then clears.

"Feel it," I say.

"Yeah, it's cold," my sister admits, begrudgingly, cautiously sticking one finger in and then drying it on her shorts, "but that doesn't mean it's fresh water. That could just be the Bay coming into your stupid hole."

"Let's get the opinion of an independent expert. Hey, Amy, look at this."

"You can't make her drink that. She'll get sick."

"I'm not going to make her drink it. She'll know."

Ahead of us, Amy stops and, like a high-wire artist, turns, her stick swinging her around with it. She drops it, licks her chops, no doubt relieved to find an excuse to spit out her trophy, and wanders over, curious. She looks at the hole with the bubbling water. I wiggle my fingers in it.

"Look, Amy: wa-wa?"

She looks, takes a tentative sip, and then guzzles it up like a college student at a keg party.

"I rest my case."

"I guess it is a spring," my sister concedes. "How'd you know?"

"They're supposed to be all around here."

A little farther down the beach, a trickle of water meanders through the sand above the high tide line, working its way to one of the tidal pools. We follow it back into the beach grass at the base of the hill to where a tiny flow runs over a shelf of hard clay.

"That? That's not a spring," Marjorie says. Look,

that's just drainage coming down from the club house."

Too late to turn back now. I stick my fingers in it.

"Ice cold! Yes!"

The "boiling springs" of the old Cape Codders. And they've been boiling for a long time. On the hilltop above this one, behind a slope, was found one of the deepest shell deposits in the area, the site of an Indian village.

Here we do turn around and head back down the beach. Like Robert Frost's traveler in the yellow wood, we'll keep for another day the beach down to the Wading Place and around to Round Pond. Holding out our arms like sails to catch the wind, we tack to windward, past the Yacht Club dock, around High Point, and then inland along the sandy path through the beach grass to the freshwater pond.

Years ago, when we first came here and this was all pitch pine woods, the tops of the tallest pines around the pond each held an enormous messy stick nest, a green heron rookery; there must have been easily forty or fifty of them then. And as we walked around the pond, hundreds of redwing blackbirds would raise a racket, darting from their nests in the cattails, then resettling. The heron left for good when the development started, and just a few families of redwing blackbirds protest our arrival today.

In from the Bay, out of the wind, the air is still, fragrant in the sun with wild pink roses climbing through the cattails and rushes that border the pond. Are the roses descendants of ones that strayed from around the old hotel? A soggy earthen path, no more than two feet wide, leads us through the swamp on one side of the pond. Overgrown on both sides with cattails that nod over our heads, the air is as humid as in a greenhouse, with all sorts of slitherings and splashes and kerplunks in the thick vegetation on either side of us as we approach. Snapping turtles? a weasel? a snake? We shiver and hurry on. Not even Amy wants to explore these ominous sounds, and hurries, double time, straight down the path, looking neither to the right nor to the left as we pass.

On a walk last summer, a great-horned owl had been perched, unseen, on a dead branch. It suddenly swooped low, straight at us, its wild yellow eyes glaring, checking to see if any of us—terrified all— might make a tasty supper. Amy never forgets to walk a little closer to us and stare up at that branch as we make our way along the path.

We come out from the shadows and cross the

road to the sun-drenched bluff overlooking Crows Pond, that lovely, almost landlocked inlet of the Bay. From the top of the bluff, we watch for a while the tiny white sailboats from Camp Avalon, the girls' sailing camp, tack back and forth. Across the pond the camp's speedboat is idling. A camper treads water at the end of the ski line. "Hit it!" we hear. The outboard roars, the line snaps tight, she's up! She's skimming across the water! She's down! The boat circles on its side back to her.

Off the beach, campers dive from the float and swim between the two docks, their shrieks and screams and laughter rising over the water. In her best dog show style, Amy prances down the beach to the camp's docks, knowing what is there: a gaggle of girls who will smother her with all their love for their pets back home.

"Amy!"

"Amy!"

"Look! It's Amy!"

"Amy!"

"Hi, Amy!"

"Amy! Here! Here!"

"Good dog, good doggy!"

"Oh, she is so beautiful!"

"Look at those eyes!"

"I know! Look! You've got the biggest, most beautiful, most brownest eyes, you know that?"

She knows, we tell them, as they kneel around her, hugging and patting her, their hero of the moment.

"Look at her little eyelashes!"

"Oh, look! They're so cute! Look! They're golden!"

"Oh, Amy, look at those eyelashes!"

"Jeepers, creepers, where'd you get those weepers?" a camper sings and jitterbugs.

"What kind of dog is it?"

"She's a golden retriever, stupid," one of the campers answers. "What do you think she is? A schnauzer?"

"My older sister has a golden retriever just like her."

Satisfied at last that she has made their day, and from the campers' delight, her satisfaction seems justified, we head on down the beach past the docks where the sand gets pebbly and then rocky under the bluffs, the remnants of the retreating glacier, which also left behind the enormous chunk of ice, stranded like a land iceberg, which melted to form this kettle hole pond. And as we round the bend past the narrow inlet in from the Bay, we hear in the pines on

Avalon Hill the crows calling back and forth, awaiting the final "Taps" a few weeks hence when these woods again will be theirs, the campers gone, the cabins boarded shut for the winter, the hulls of the sailboats overturned on the field next to the rec hall.

Suddenly, Amy's amblings from tide line to beach grass to Bay and back into the scrub growth becomes directed. Her dog radar has honed in on something ahead. *Dead sand shark! Dead sand shark! Dead sand shark!* must be pinging in her brain as she races straight toward a suspicious lump in the mat of eelgrass down by the water, sniffs it, and then slides right into it with heavenly delight. Up again, and then another divine slide. That's right, get it real good right in there behind the ears where it'll stink for days.

"Amy, that is so gross!"

"Oh Amy, no! No! Amy, no!"

She looks at us with a dazed expression of satiation, shakes, and then proceeds on, pleased with her new scent.

"Ohhh, gross me out!"

"She stinks!"

"The campers wouldn't even get within a mile of her now."

"You've got to wash her!"

"I'm not touching her. That's disgusting."

"Here. At least get her to go in the water. That should get some of it off."

"Amy, here," my father calls, knowing no one else will do the really dirty work.

With the tips of his fingers, he unbuckles her blue collar, reeking of week-old rotting sand shark. I take a piece of driftwood and throw it out into the inlet.

In she goes to retrieve, as my father rubs her collar in the sand and then rinses it back and forth in the saltwater.

Amy swims in, shakes off, rolls on her back in the sand, pausing for a delicious moment to let the sun warm her belly, then lies down to start chewing her piece of driftwood.

A cautious, four person sniff test does not result in a single passing grade, so the driftwood is pried from her mouth and into the water it goes again, this time a little farther out, followed by an odiferous retriever who dutifully retrieves it. She shakes, driftwood still in mouth, and then starts on down the beach toward home as if to say, *Enough nonsense; this is pretty expensive perfume and now it's being ruined by all the saltwater.*

One by one we've taken off our windbreakers and tied them around our waists. Here, in the lee of

Avalon Hill, there's not a ripple on the water, just the gentle heave of the tide; but out beyond Fox Hill Island, the fishing boats leaving Ryder's Cove hit the swells as they get past the channel markers, and farther out the Bay is rough with whitecaps.

Rounding the beach past Fox Hill, we face the wind again, where on this point of land exposed to all the winds once stood the saltworks. From old photographs, the windmills, which pumped water up from the Bay to evaporate in long shallow wooden troughs, looked like junior high school science projects, built without any parental assistance, but they did the trick. By the War of 1812, when cannon were dragged in from Boston to protect these operations from the British, Chatham had eighty saltworks around the shores of the Bay, creaking and clacking, pumping away; but by the late nineteenth century, the discovery of salt mines in Syracuse, New York, ended the industry.

Comfortably tired, we wearily trudge the beach heading home, closing our eyes and inhaling the nourishing northwest wind that once turned the arms of the windmills. Feeling like sailors reaching port after a long voyage, we climb the sandy path to the lawn and tumble into the white wooden chairs on top of the bluff:

Home is the sailor, home from the sea,
And the hunter home from the hill.

For a while, we watch shadows of clouds hurry across the lawn, and the catboat pulling at its mooring, and gulls dipping and soaring above the channel. Amy sits under the pines looking toward the Bay, her eyes half shut, then closed, then open again, until she lies down in the shade, dozing and dreaming, listening to the steady sigh of the breeze through the pines and the faraway roar of the surf on the outerbeach.

That was then, Amy. Do you hear it now, in the October wind in the hemlocks outside the front door? In the oak leaves blowing about the lawn?

And all I ask,
And all I ask is a windy day with the white
clouds flying . . .

I wish we'd had time to explore some more of the beaches around the Bay, Amy. The whole west shore, you would have liked that. We could have left the car down at a town landing and walked up the beach past the Narrows between the headland and Sipson Island and in around Little Pleasant Bay. Hog Island is back in there, with Money Head on one end, where Captain Kidd is said to have buried treasure. Some fisherman in 1946 found a stash of old coins there. Really. It was in the *National Geographic*. And in there around Quanset Pond and Namequoit, that's where the pines are thick right down to the beach, and those salt meadows in toward Meeting House Pond, you'd have liked it in there, too.

But the beach at Scatteree was good, wasn't it? Up around Minister's Point where we would watch the trawlers chugging back to harbor in the late afternoon sun with clouds of gulls around them, calling and calling. Remember that? And the lighthouse beach where the ocean waves come through the inlet and right in to shore and you could feel the cool breath of the sea.

There were a lot of great walks, weren't there? The ones along Harding Beach on those smoky days when the southwest wind churned up the Sound and the sandpipers, like mechanical wind-up toys, scurried ahead of us where the waves were breaking over each other. Along the beach at Morris Island where the sand was so white and the bay translucent sea-lettuce green and off in the distance you could see the shimmering sands of Monomoy, the Cape Mallebarre of the early explorers. And through the woods of Watchung Reservation right here, don't forget that, that's where we would have gone this morning, over the wooden footbridge across the stream, up the side of the ravine, through the dark forest of tall pine and oak: that was really good wolf country, wasn't it?

But always among our best walks were those closest to home, where the frontier lay just beyond our doorstep.

Chapter Four

Roughhousing

*R*emember the summer storms? We always knew they were brewing if the wind was blowing up the leaves of the poplars along the shore when we took our morning walks. I know, you knew because dogs just know those things in their own ways.

Remember how all day it would feel like a storm was coming in? And the small craft warning flag would be flying at the lighthouse?

It's dusk now. The sky and Bay are timber wolf gray. Packs of waves with livid whitecap fangs race and leap down the channel, snapping and biting at Dogfish Bar and trying to tear loose from its mooring our frightened catboat. These waves mean business. We've been caught out in them before and know they want to kill. As I look up from my book out the picture window in the sunroom, I think of the director of the sailing camp down the Bay, who had sailed these waters for forty years; he was out in his Sailfish when waves like these picked up. It was several days before his body was found on the backside of one of the islands. No, better be snug inside when a nor'easter howls in from the sea.

On the wall of the sunroom, the wind indicator light glowers orange, flashing north, northeast, north, northeast, east, northeast. Now rain lunges at the picture window, pounces on the roof, growls through the gutters.

"Someone take Amy out," my mother calls from the kitchen. "She hasn't been out since this morning."

My father is in the den with the game on. I look over at Marjorie, curled up asleep on the loveseat. Amy is luxuriously stretched out on the carpet, dozing and listening to the storm.

It's my turn, I know, but it's worth a try anyhow.

"Your mother wants someone to take the dog out," I say to Marjorie.

It's your turn," she mumbles from somewhere far away, her eyes closed shut.

It is, so I don't press the issue.

Okay, Amy, it's us," I say, reluctantly laying down *The Widow's Walk* and getting out of that particularly comfortable old Victorian rocker, the one that had been in my great grandmother's apartment, the upholstered one with the big springs under the wooden rockers. Just thinking of going out in the storm I can feel the claws of rain scratching at the back of my neck. "We're going to brave this gale and go out there and do our business, right Amy?"

Amy doesn't budge. Having learned from the master, she closes her eyes, just like Marjorie, and feigns deep sleep.

"Okay, Amy, here we go!" I say, trying to make it sound like an adventure.

For a water dog who will splash into the Bay any time, any season, Amy abhors a sprinkle of rain on her head. To even think of going out in a nor'easter clearly is out of the question. She's nestled in for the duration.

"What? Are you like some big old house cat, afraid to get wet?" I ask in utter amazement. "A big old Maine coon pussy cat?"

A cheap trick, but that catches her attention. Without too much enthusiasm, she raises up just enough to look toward the picture window to see if there really is—and she does have serious doubts about this—a cat dumb enough to be outside in the pouring rain.

Let's get this done, whatever it takes, I think to myself, anxious to go out, come in, dry off and get back to my mystery. Maybe it's time for an old-fashioned cat scare.

I rush up to the window and look out at the storm. "It is a *cat!*" I call to Amy with concern. "A *big cat!*"

From drowsy slumber to red alert in an instant, she's up and at the window, looking. *Where? Where?*

Cat scares are getting a little old, but just often enough there actually is a suspicious-looking cat out there, lurking across the lawn stalking the quail. So it is essential for us to check out each alarm. We race from the sunroom through the living room, picking up speed as we pass through the kitchen with Amy's toenails skating over the floor. In the breezeway I grab an umbrella, and we're out on the patio, Amy at attention, looking here and there in the deluge for a sight of the evil, soggy feline intruder.

"There. I saw it there!" I say, pointing out to the bluff with my umbrella held against the wind blowing the rain straight in at the house.

The sounds of wind whipping through the pines and waves tearing down the channel and rain lashing against the house mix in a menacing howl.

"Hurry," I urge Amy, "hurry!"

Amy senses she might have been tricked but, as not to lose face, trots out to the top of the bluff, gives a perfunctory look around for trouble, and then, finding none and knowing I'm watching intently, at least goes through a pantomime of doing what she's supposed to do (a pantomime I'm convinced on occasion she performs to get those who are obsessively concerned with her bodily functions off her back). Then, her ears blowing about like wind socks, lickety-split, she tears back to the shelter of the house.

I lock the door behind us against the storm.

In the breezeway she gives a good, deliberate head to tail shake, spraying off the rain. And that is that. She heads back to the sunroom, dark now but for the light from the table lamp by my rocker, and resumes her nap which has been so rudely interrupted.

"Did you dry her with a towel?" my mother calls from the kitchen a few minutes after I'm settled in the rocker and am back into my Nantucket murder mystery.

"What?"

"Did you dry the dog with a towel?"

"Damn," I mutter.

"Make sure her chest is dry," my mother reminds me as I walk out to the back hall to get from the bottom of the closet the old orange bath towel. "The chest is the most important part to get bone dry."

Now, since the time when man first invited dog to come live in his house, there has always been a lot of give and take in making this cross-species relationship work. At times, the relationship can be so close that we believe dogs are very much like us, that we, indeed, are related, that we're parents or children, brothers or sisters. And dogs, studies have shown, watch us and know us better than we know them. Maybe dogs find that we become more like them, and maybe we do. They adopt us into their packs as we adopt them into our families. Yet there will always be things about dogs we just cannot comprehend, like what it is that is so ecstatically delightful in sliding into something dead and smelly and squishing it up real tight behind the ears, just as there must be many things about us that dogs cannot fathom, like the endless idle hours we spend seated before the flickering images in a big black box.

With few exceptions, what Amy might not fully understand she gamely accepts. And one of those few exceptions is getting toweled dry. For the supreme leader of a pack to be dried off behind the ears and have her tummy rubbed dry after being outside in the rain is, to her, completely incomprehensible and un-reasonable. Clearly it is unacceptable.

Carrying the orange bath towel into the sunroom is like pirouetting with a red cape through the streets of Pamplona during the running of the bulls. As soon as Amy sees it coming, she charges it, grabbing hold of a corner, and, hanging on, shakes it like a partridge.

She has her end, I have mine, with which I quickly go to work.

"Oh, nice and dry, we're going to get you so nice and dry," I singsong chant, toweling under each ear and around her throat. "Ohhhhh, so beautiful, such beautiful, lovely, luscious golden hair, so soft and silky, lustrous honey blonde hair, uummm, so smooth and soft."

Nodding slowly in agreement, she momentarily succumbs to this soothing beautyshop lullaby, almost letting her end of the towel drop from her mouth.

She catches herself just as it does, and grabs it with a snap.

"Amy get dry," I patiently explain, prying open her jaws and pulling out the gooey end, only to have her lunge for another hunk of it.

She looks up at me to see how I'm taking it.

"Now wait a minute," I indignantly protest. "Wait just a minute! They wouldn't put up with this in a beauty parlor, and you know it."

With her hanging on to one end of the towel, all the while slyly waiting to reel in more if I relax my hold on it, I work with the few square inches of towel she's left me, drying around the ears, under the chin, down the chest, the back, the tail, the legs, rolling her over on her back to get the stomach. Swishing her tail back and forth, her black lips grinning, she grabs more towel, which she holds in her jaws and flails with her paws.

"This is so silly, Amy. Why would a dog even think of something like this? What would a dog? What would a dog even be thinking?" I ask Amy in astonishment as she rolls back over on her stomach, tugging at her end of the towel and staring right at me, defiantly.

"What's she doing?" Marjorie asks, wide awake now that all the dirty work has been done and the fun might be beginning.

"I think she's being defiant. To me, at least," I say, tugging at my end of the towel to get more back, "this smacks of defiance. Do we have to take it?"

"No we do not," Marjorie states empathically, descending from the loveseat to the carpet to the scene of impending battle. "Give me that end."

And the games begin.

"Is she dry?" my mother calls in, not fully appreciating the enormity of the task she has assigned. To her, Amy always is a little girl who could be dressed up in ribbons and ruffles for tea parties, a sweet little girl all sugar and spice and everything nice.

"Yup. As dry as she's going to get," I answer.

"Did you get the chest? The chest is most important."

"It's as dry as I can get it."

I neglect to report that our beauty parlor patron is currently engaged in a rousing game of tug-of-war, with Marjorie manning the other end of the orange towel.

Already the game is getting pretty intense.

"Amy, you're a brute and you know it," Marjorie says.

All golden retrievers like to fantasize that they can be fierce, and Amy redoubles her tugging.

"Come on, one hand," I tell my sister. "Give her a chance."

"Give her a chance? Give her a chance?" she hisses at me, hanging on to the towel for dear life. "This is not a retriever you brought back in. This is some kind of wolf dog that's loose in the house."

And sure enough, Amy's lovely and loving brown eyes have assumed the frightening steely glint of the Big Bad Wolf's eyes in that split second when Little Red Riding Hood suddenly perceived that it was not Grandmama under the covers.

"One hand, one hand, those are the rules," I remind her again. "She's only got one mouth."

"Okay, okay," my sister mutters, letting go with one hand and instantly losing several inches of towel as Amy pulls back against the momentary slack.

"I told you! She's not playing fair."

"She's playing fair, and she's going to beat you if you don't watch out."

Now the match gets serious, and a gambling man in that dark room with the wind wailing about the eaves would have had a hard time knowing where to place his bet: on a Wellesley graduate sprawled on the floor, one end of a towel clenched in her hand, pulling for all she was worth, or on a wily retriever with the other end of the towel clenched in bared teeth, her eyes becoming more and more demonic, a low warning rumbling from her throat, watching, watching, waiting for that split second of weakness, a moment of exhaustion, a repositioning,

Now!

In a movement almost too quick to see, Amy lets

go of the towel and pounces on it several inches closer to the middle, an ominous growl in her throat defying anyone to call that cheating; and is that a look of triumph in her eyes?

"See! I told you! That's cheating!" my sister declares.

Bully on you, Amy seems to reply as she repeats her tactic and lunges again at the towel, grabbing it inches from my sister's fingers.

Marjorie lets go as if she touched a mouse crouched in the dusty dark corner of a cupboard and jumps back out of the way.

"Good gods, Amy, you win. Okay? I quit. You win. You can have the stupid towel. It's yours."

Amy already knows she has won without waiting for that gracious concession speech. She grabs my sister's end of the towel, lying over the rest of it, and begins a methodical ripping, viciously shaking a hunk.

Game over, right? Amy has won fair and square, everyone is ready to concede that. But woe be unto whoever tries to retrieve that towel. This is the really hard part of the game.

Left to her devices, Amy will make a great show of angrily ripping loose every thread of the hated towel, mash around a bunch until they're nice and soggy, and then swallow, which isn't good for the drying towel or for a golden retriever. Our mission impossible is to take the towel away and let it dry out for another rainy day.

"Here, get the towel," I breezily tell my sister as if it's the simplest matter in the world.

"Are you crazy? I'm not going near it," she says from the safety of the loveseat, her bare feet tucked under her. "You get it."

Amy is waiting for just such an eventuality, her eyes challenging anyone who comes within five feet of her. Any closer and she lets go of the towel and assumes her protective position, huddling over it, trying to get a more threatening look in her eye, closer still and a warning snarl, then a wrinkling of the nose, a show of fierce retriever teeth, the hair on the back of her neck magically rises, and if anyone is foolish enough to lay even a finger on a stray corner of that towel, Attack! the most ferocious, fiercest, most bloodcurdling snarl and lunge at those misplaced fingers as if she meant to tear them out at the roots.

Amy never actually connects with human flesh, perhaps because she doesn't really intend to and is merely training us to be fair. Or perhaps she is just having some fun bullying us (she always seems to chuckle to herself as soon as she snarls and, like the gracious winner of a heated tennis match, trots right over to shake hands). Or maybe under these circumstances of imminent peril, misplaced human fingers can retreat pretty quickly. But her response always is the same. And, upon reflection, it does make sense: she has won the game, fair and square. The trophy is hers. That is retriever fairness. And who could argue with that?

But there is still the matter of getting the towel back while it still resembles a towel and not merely its constituent threads. As Mr. Darling in *Peter Pan* learned with Nana, all the sweet talk in the world will get you nowhere. Fair, after all, is fair. To the victor belong the spoils.

It's time to play our trump card: cheese.

Like old Ben Gunn marooned on Treasure Island, Amy dreams of cheese, long, sweet, deliciously repetitive dreams of cheese. For a good morsel of cheese, there isn't anything she won't do.

We know it will work.

"Would you like a little piece of cheese?" we ask as she glares at us, awaiting our next move.

She looks at us, suspiciously, considering our offer, still holding the towel firmly in clenched jaws, not about to be fooled by the old Trojan Horse ploy.

"No, really. A little bit of *cheese?*"

It always helps to describe exactly what kind of cheese we're talking about.

"We've got some of that new sharp cheddar *cheese*. Yup, the strong kind. From Vermont. It's pretty good *cheese*."

The towel is dropped, long forgotten, the last thing on her mind. Who wants a dry, tasteless towel when there's cheese being distributed?

She's up. She's herding us toward the kitchen six inches from our legs, faster, faster. *Must get that cheese.*

Into the bright kitchen she skips, as sweet and innocent as little Miss Muffet, her wolf mask put away. Straight to the refrigerator where fabulous stashes of cheese are stored. Out comes the slab of golden cheese from the back of the refrigerator door. It is laid on the counter. Two brown eyes watch in salivating anticipation, like Ben Gunn's, as it is placed on a breadboard, the wrapper opened, a paring knife taken from a drawer, a nice hunk neatly cut from it and, like a pirate's gold bar, divided into thirds.

"What's that for?" my mother asks.

"We had to promise her cheese to get the towel back," my sister explains.

"Oh, don't be ridiculous," my mother responds. "She always lets me dry her, don't you, Amy? Amy, you have them buffaloed, that's what I think."

A tasty morsel of strong Vermont cheddar cheese, down the hatch in a gulp. And a healthy half of the other two pieces from the tug-of-war losers.

Pots bubble and simmer on the stove. The smell of chicken roasting in the oven catches Amy's interest. She looks up at my mother, expectantly, as if to ask, *Is there anything I can do to help in the kitchen? Is it ready yet?* Can I have a piece now? Amy knows by heart the answers to each of these kitchen questions, but her philosophy is that it never hurts to ask. And she knows, too, that at dinnertime, merely by resting her head in our laps and poking her nose into the stomachs of those pack members she can so easily dominate, she will secure all the chicken she wants, no hunting or skinning required.

Our work is done. We're in for the night, cozy and warm. The orange towel is out of sight, having been secreted in the washing machine. Everyone is content. We three head back to the sunroom to resume our dozing and sleeping and reading, as outside the wind drives sheets of rain against the house as if the storm will blow all night.

Chapter Five

Baywatch

A summer afternoon. The old catboat sleeps at its mooring. Over the islands, a small white cloud drifts slowly toward the outerbeach where the heat haze shimmers above the dunes.

"Let's go swimming," someone suggests.

"Now?" comes a doubtful reply.

"Is the tide right?" another wonders.

"It's perfect. Coming in. Half in. More than half in. Come on!"

We don our bathing suits, faded from summers past, grab some beach towels and, single file, follow Amy along the sandy path down the bluff, past the scraggly salt-spray rose and bayberry, fragrant in the baking sun, to the beach.

Yes! they're finally doing something, Amy no doubt is thinking, delighted to lead us on a new adventure.

From experience we know an unchaperoned beach blanket is fair game for Amy, who will snatch it and race down the beach, or, if that doesn't precipitate an enthusiastic chase, lie down with a good portion of it safely wedged under her and proceed, methodically, to rip it to shreds, daring anyone to try to rescue it. So we drop our towels in the rowboat pulled up in the beach grass, and slip off our Top-Siders and sandals and stash them under the seat (as Amy notes for future reference their exact whereabouts if things get dull), and then hopscotch over the scorching sand, onto the mats of crinkly dried eelgrass, to the water's edge.

It's a quiet time of day, a timeless time of day, an afternoon in the middle of the summer in the middle of the week. The Bay is still, with just a pulse at its surface as the flood tide pushes the water through the channel between the beach and Strong Island. The shorebirds are away, waiting wherever they wait for the tide to ebb so that again they can harvest the flats. Off Minister Point, the boats nod and bob at their moorings, awaiting their weekend sailors.

With the sun warming our backs and the clear water cooling our feet, we watch for a while, hypnotized, the tide coming through the channel and the white cloud drifting out toward the ocean.

At last, we take a step in.

"Stout hearts, me laddy bucks," one of us is sure to say, echoing my grandfather's words when we had gone swimming here with him years before, over thirty-five years ago now, the summer before he built his retirement home on the bluff.

"Is it cold?" we ask our leader.

My mother, who has already waded up to her knees, shakes her head no. "It's like soup."

And the first few steps through the shallows where the schools of silversides dart away from our shadows are as delightfully warm as the womblike waters where life began.

On a hot summer day like today, the Bay never feels cold once we take that first plunge and start swimming. Yet for some reason, as we wade in, the water temperature does seem to change from heavenly to cooler, and then, as we proceed out, step by cautious step and the water rises a touch above the knees. "It's freezing!" my father or I cry out, cringing and retreating a step. It feels like we're standing right at the exit point of one of those underwater springs.

"Don't be ridiculous," my mother replies, not all that convincingly as she delicately splashes her hands around in the water and dabs just a touch on her face. "You just have to get used to it."

Used to it? Water lapping against stomach skin seems a particularly cruel form of torture.

With the incoming tide, a clump of seaweed brushes my leg, reminding me of that brochure about the old Hotel Chatham and the comforting guarantee about "drainage and plumbing" that had been penned by the chief engineer who devised its modern system: "The system of sewage of the Hotel Chatham was designed by us and constructed under our supervision with the object of securing an absolutely safe and inoffensive removal of all the liquid wastes. By its means all sewage is quietly removed to a distance from the building, and at the proper time discharged into the swift current of the ebb tide, and carried out to sea."

I do some quick calculations. The last flush of one of the hotel's "arsenals" had been a good ninety years ago. The tide is coming in, at least three hours in. Should be okay.

"I don't know about this," I wonder out loud, just checking to see if any of the others are growing faint of heart. "I don't think it's warmed up enough yet. Maybe we should wait for the tide to start going out."

"Pifflesticks," my mother responds. And probably she is right. The inlet is a mile down the Bay, around past the headland of Minister's Point, and it does make logical sense that the flood tide would bring in the frigid waters of the North Atlantic. But the truth is that the ebb tide, which again, logically, should be warmer from its leisurely journey around the islands and over the sand flats and shoal waters of the upper Bay, on its return always seems just as cold.

"Women have extra fat deposits that keep them warm," my father explains to me confidentially, looking like he is ready to pack it in and head back to the house; "that's why they don't feel the cold as much."

My mother brushes aside his remark, as if flicking off a pesky greenhead fly, and continues wading out.

Amy is searching the shallows, fascinated by the activity she sees in a tidal pool, looking here and there as pogies in a frenzy flash helter-skelter about her legs, staring at a spider crab emerging from underneath a clump of seaweed, putting her nose right in the water and blowing bubbles as she looks to see if that indeed is a tasty morsel of old clam at the bottom, all the while with the concerned expression of an elderly babysitter at a playground, watching the bizarre and tragic human spectacle unfolding before her.

"Hey, Amy. Look at this."

I pull from the water by its long hard tail a horseshoe crab that had been scuttling along past my feet and hold it up for her to see, its four sets of legs wiggling every which way, its gills flapping in protest at so rude an introduction.

Amy wades out to take a look at it, curious, coming closer, but not too close, not at all sure what to make of this strange creature.

Not a crab at all but a distant relative of the spider family, and an elderly relative at that, this, the oldest living fossil, is a direct descendant of creatures that, just like it, scuttled across the floors of the bays and estuaries and marshes of 350 million years ago. Fossils have shown that so perfect was the horseshoe crab at creation that it has not had to evolve since then, surviving, thriving, through all the great climatic changes the world has seen, through the ice ages, the meteor showers, the volcanic explosions, the earthquakes, through the many alterations in its food supply, through all of man's meddling.

The Indians around the Bay fashioned horseshoe crab tails into arrowheads, farmers later used their carcasses for fertilizer and chicken feed, and fishermen cut them up as bait for their eel and conch traps. Not so many years ago, some of the towns around the Bay put a bounty of a penny a tail on the horseshoe crab since it was believed to be a voracious consumer of seed softshell clams and quahogs.

It's only been in the last few years that the importance of these creatures has been recognized. Its main diet turned out not to be shellfish after all, but rather the dead organic matter on the floor of marshes and bays: nature's vacuum cleaners. Some towns have begun paying suppliers to reintroduce them into their waters. And scientists have discovered that the blue, copper-based blood of the horseshoe crab contains an extraordinarily effective antibiotic system, which they have been able to use to produce a serum to detect the presence of bacteria in human blood, contamination in pharmaceutical products, and spinal meningitis in children. And that's not all. Its blue blood is being used in AIDS and Alzheimer's neurobiological research. The tails might have been going for a penny apiece when I was growing up, but their blood sells today for upward of fifteen thousand dollars a quart.

No matter how remarkable is this prehistoric relic swimming at full speed away from us, Amy is not about to be distracted for long from her lifeguard duties.

My mother's foolhardy march to sea—she is now up to her waist and is seriously considering the fateful next move—has put Amy on alert: she stands in the shallows staring at the tragedy about to take place before her very eyes, aghast at my mother's plight.

"Well, there's no time like the present," my mother

says bravely, snapping on her bathing cap and, to show us how cowardly we are, plunging in and swimming parallel to shore with her measured crawl.

That's it.

A burst of spray!

A dramatic leap or two to deeper water.

And Amy is on her way, chugging out to my mother like a tugboat in overdrive, her back arching out of the water with each powerful pull of her paws. She's out at the scene of the tragedy before my mother has taken two or three strokes.

Amy positions herself on the deep side, the dangerous side, of this prostrate form, and with rather frantic whining noises and a determined look in her eyes, tries valiantly to herd her closer to shore, swimming tighter and tighter circles around her.

Once actually in, the water feels delightful, and my mother turns over on her back for a float down the Bay with the current.

"Perfect!" she calls to us, waving enthusiastically.

Is it really, we wonder, or is this a sneaky ploy to lure us in to suffer with her? Another step out and we suspect the worst.

A lifeguard's warnings should never be ignored.

Amy grabs for whatever flesh is available, in this case, an ear lobe.

"Ouch!" my mother cries, standing up and moving in closer to shore until she reaches the exact depth Amy feels is just right for her swimming competence, at which point, her job done, Amy swims to shore, shakes off, and shakes her head in amazement that any member of her pack could be so reckless. Satisfied with another successful rescue, she rolls in the sand, and then watches to make sure the menfolk are not as demented.

Of course we are. One by one, the men, now shamed, shivering in the summer sun, tense their muscles, take the plunge, breathe deeply to make certain they have not suffered cardiac arrest, and then set off down the Bay with Amy swimming beside us on the deep side, amazed at our stupidity, warning us to stay close to shore.

On the flood tide, the incoming waters of the Bay have to funnel through the narrow channel between the beach and Strong Island, which creates a powerful current through this passage. From the top of the bluff we often can see the water pushing through before it spreads out into the Bay and slows down with a sigh as it loses speed. Riding this current is as luxurious a feeling as sleep swimming. With an easy breaststroke or crawl, we can effortlessly pick up the speed of an Olympic swimmer, watching the shoreline zip by. Going back against it, we struggle to gain every foot; and if we pause for just a moment, we'll lose it all and then some.

With the current so strong here, this point of land would have been an improbable spot on which to construct a naval air station to guard the coast during World War I. So the government, of course, built one right here, with enormous hangars for seaplanes and dirigibles, quarters for the servicemen back in the woods by Crows Pond, repair shops, a mess hall, and a water tank. The light seaplanes hauled from their hangers above the beach and out into the middle of the channel were carried by the current halfway down the Bay before they could even get their propellors humming. And the wind! Like the winds that bore down on the raft of Odysseus, the winds here, having gained strength over unobstructed miles of open sea, race across the sandy elbow of this peninsula thrust thirty miles out into the Atlantic. "If you don't like the weather," old Cape

Codders have said, "wait a few minutes." And there's a lot of truth to that. Clouds are blown across open sky, pushed together hiding the sun, and spun apart again. Tempests explode in momentary furies, cracking open the heavens, and just as quickly pass. On this spit of land swept by sea winds, the dirigibles didn't stand a chance; on most days, the wind blew them all over the place.

Three of the pilings from the old Navy dock that extended into the Bay where we are swimming still stand on the beach, a foot above the sand, tilting at crazy angles, worn and splintery and encrusted with ancient barnacles. And here and there back in the undergrowth are slabs of concrete—parts of the bases of the seaplane and blimp hangers—all that remains of the fortifications against an enemy that never came.

Except once.

It was a peaceful summer Sunday morning—July 21, 1918—a hot summer day just like today, when right off the ocean beach at Orleans, a stone's throw out in the water, the periscope of a 213-foot submarine of the Imperial German Navy broke the glassy surface of the sea.

No doubt the Kaiser's sailors were itching for a little fun, but there was nothing in sight for target practice save a puny tugboat hauling four empty barges. Oh well. Ready? Aim . . . Fire!

At ten thirty that morning, U156 let loose a torpedo at the tiny convoy and then began lobbing in shells. Hundred of townspeople and vacationers rushed to the dunes to watch the action, as one by one the barges sank and the tug's wheelhouse was blown off.

The Orleans Coast Guard Station wired the Chatham Naval Air Station: Help!

Most of the Air Station's flyboys, however, were up in Provincetown playing in a Sunday morning ball game. Nevertheless, the men still at the Station dragged four double-pontoon mahogany-hulled seaplanes from their hangers into the Bay, brought aboard their pigeons in case the newfangled radios didn't work, taxied down the channel, and took off up the coast.

The airmen soon spotted the menacing shape of the U-boat, but there was one problem: their seaplanes were unarmed. The only officer with the key to the bomb fuse locker at the Air Station being the catcher that morning in the ball game at Provincetown.

The seaplanes buzzed the U-boat and, in frustration, one pilot threw a monkey wrench at it. Reports differ, some saying he scored a bull's-eye, the monkey wrench banging into the German war machine; others note that the monkey wrench splashed into the sea. Whichever report was accurate, it seems certain that the chuckles of Kapitan-Lieutenant Von Oldenberg and his crew echoed in U156 as it slipped safely beneath the waves, in this the first, and only, enemy attack upon the United States in World War I.

No dirigibles watch over the coast today, just a fluffy summer cloud drifting above us as we float on our backs down the Bay. And the U156 is long gone; three months after its attack on the tugboat, it hit a mine in the North Sea and sank. The only bombing raids now are the gulls that at low tide drop scallops on the slab of concrete up in the beach grass, the remnants of an old seaplane hanger. And the only armed beach patrol is a watchdog, soaked and sleek as an otter, searching not for spies and saboteurs but pacing the beach to make certain her pack members don't go out beyond their depth.

Far down from where we started floating, we stand and wade back against the current, step by step, the water rushing by our legs, back to where we set out, and then float back down again with just a flick of our hands and an occasional flutter of our feet, going back again and again as if on an amusement park ride. Finally, tired and waterlogged and thinking in our human simplemindedness that we can always do it again tomorrow afternoon, even after learning, time and again through years of experience, that rarely are the conditions just right when we're ready, finally, like some ungodly form of prehistoric life emerging from the ancient seas, we stumble up the beach to our towels in the rowboat.

Relieved that at last we've come to our senses, Amy does a quick head count, then races up the path to the lawn, where, after rolling on the grass, we'll find her — our Lassie, our Rin-Tin-Tin — lying on her back warming her stomach in the sun.

Not such a bad idea. Refreshed, we sit for a while in the wooden chairs on the bluff, feeling the pleasant warmth of the afternoon sun, watching the flood tide surge between island and beach.

Chapter Six

Over the Bounding Main

Hey, Amy, how about that time we went sailing? Oh, I know, you'd like to forget about that, right? But it turned out okay, you have to admit that. And I bet if you'd have given it another chance, you would have been a first-class seadog. Lots of retrievers are into boating. Maybe you were too young. What were you—five or six months old then? But it was a really calm day. Remember?

The warm southwest wind off Nantucket Sound is the prevailing summer wind, and in the afternoons it can pick up with gusts of twenty blowing flat out across the Bay and then you can do some pretty exciting sailing. That will come later. This morning (it's one of those days at the end of August when you try to pretend the summer isn't over), as I row our passengers out to the mooring for Amy's maiden voyage, it's so calm you can hear drops of water fall from the blades of the oars.

The small catboat waits docilely at its mooring, the reflection of its white hull and dark green trim nodding beside it in the still water. Our dinghy gently touches.

I tie the painter to the mooring can; after Marjorie climbs into the boat, I lift Amy up to her.

"Quite a catch you have there, Captain. Tuna or shark?"

"There'll be some mighty juicy fillets tonight, me laddy buck, simmered to perfection in a fine Madeira."

"Oh, Amy, he doesn't mean it," Marjorie says, placing her hands over Amy's ears. "Actually, she'd make a terrific hammerhead shark," she adds, intoning the shark's theme from *Jaws* and pushing back Amy's lips to reveal the pearly teeth, dear, tiny, and sharp as carpet tacks: *"Bom bombom bom bombom."*

Amy stands on the seat and shakes herself, a leisurely shake that starts at her head and travels to the tip of her tail, splattering us.

"Hey!" we cry out.

She looks at us and flashes a retriever grin.

"Fetch the cat-o'-nine tails, Matey; this lubber needs a dressing down."

"A court-martial first when we reach port. Due process, don't you know?"

Amy shows no concern whatsoever about appearing before any such tribunal. Why should she? Just by giving the judge and jury adoring looks, she's always been found not guilty of some of the most heinous offenses. She pokes around the boat, sniffing the salt-soaked wood and lines bleached white by the sun.

"Stow the gear below deck, me laddy buck," I say to Marjorie, handing her the paddle, the life cushions, and the canvas bag filled with sunglasses, suntan lotion, a beach blanket, cameras, and in case we're becalmed, a few biscuits and a bottle of water.

"This stupid boat doesn't have a below deck."

"Belay that talk or I'll cut your ration of hardtack. A double ration for our newseaman."

"And don't do all that stupid sailor talk with Amy," Marjorie grouses. "She doesn't know what the hell you're jabbering about. Look how nervous you're making her."

"Okay, Amy, okay. But you know, sailors come aboard this ship as boys, and after a turn or two at the capstan's bar, by the time we bring 'em back to port, they're men."

"Amy doesn't want to be a man."

"Well, she can be a passenger this time, out for a morning's sail."

Without even an offer of assistance from passenger or crew, I haul the line that lifts the sail. The creaking of the pulleys and the flop-flapping of the pile of canvas rising up from the boom to the tip of the mast has our passenger frantically searching for a lifeboat.

"Amy, it's okay. See? It's just a sail."

I might just as well have been explaining to her how the boat, with a modern system of water-tight compartments, is virtually unsinkable: she's ready to abandon ship and take her chances. She stands on the seat, looking to shore, hoping, perhaps, that a more sensible, older pack member will run down to the beach and save her from this lunacy.

"Hurry up," my sister complains. "See, you're making her nervous."

"Here, lower the centerboard."

"And get my hands ripped off? No way I'm touching that thing."

"Okay," I say calmly, giving her the mainsail line, "hold this."

She takes hold of it as if it were the hairless pink tippy end of a rat's tail.

I untie fthe centerboard line from its cleat and lower the centerboard carefully, inch by inch, demonstrating by example that one's hands need not necessarily be ripped off in the process if the procedure is executed properly. Then, with the quiet professionalism of an old salt, I lean over the bow, untie the boat from its mooring, cast off, walk back to the stern, sit next to the tiller, take the line from Marjorie, pull in the sail and steer out toward the channel.

First-class passenger Amy is not at all impressed by this flawless display of seamanship. In fact, she stares, panic-stricken, at her house, her home, the entire world she knows, separated from her by a good fifty feet of open water.

And the crew! The crew is mutinous.

"Is this stupid thing even moving?" Marjorie demands.

"Yes, of course. Look at the mooring."

She looks quite skeptically at the blue-and-white mooring can with the dinghy tied to it. It is indeed astern of us, though, I admit, not by much.

"Can't you make it go any faster? I haven't got all day."

"Lan'lubbers," I mumble under my breath, hauling in the sail a bit.

"What?"

"No, I cannot get it moving any faster. Surprising though this may be, the wind is beyond our control."

"Well this is no good," she concludes with a huff, adjusting one of the life cushions behind her and settling back, spreading her arms out on either side of the deck and closing her eyes.

The only sounds are the water chuckling and gurgling in the centerboard well, and if you listen closely, the soft swish of the boat moving through the water. And in a few minutes I notice her facial muscles relaxing and I'm not sure if she is dozing yet or not.

Not all passengers are confident enough of their captain's credentials to fall asleep. Not about to be lulled into any false sense of security, Amy is pacing, looking for a safe spot to hide from the disaster she is convinced is imminent, squiggling in between the back of my legs and the transom. I can feel her trembling.

The sail catches what little there is of the light morning breeze; and almost imperceptibly, we're lazing down the channel with the outgoing tide, with just enough wind in the sail to steer.

Broadbeamed and slow, the sailboat lumbers along like a big drowsy bear, by Strong Island, the largest of the Bay's necklace of glacial islands, by its hills covered with pitch pine, by the guest house almost hidden now behind the trees. There's supposed to be a treasure chest buried on the outerbeach "northeast of a grove of trees on Strong Island," and I always scan the island for an unusual tree or two. These instructions are worthless, I conclude once again; the whole island now is pines, solid pines, nothing but pines, and all seem the same height. No "tall tree near Spy-glass Hill" here, as there was on Treasure Island, though the Bay, in the seventeenth century called Sutcliffe's Inlet, is rumored to have been a rendezvous of early New England pirates.

We amble by the sandy bluff at the island's eastern end, blunted by long-ago battles with the sea; below the bluff, the enormous marsh, larger than the island, wades far out into the Bay.

The marsh looks like acres and acres of wet green, but staring at it as we slip slowly by, it begins to appear more like a subtle impressionistic painting, a patchwork of color and texture: the blending shades of green of salt meadow grass and rushes and reeds turning yellow and straw gold, with a maze of blue creeks meandering through.

At the end of the summer in the old days, the

townspeople would pole wide, flat-bottomed scows out to these marshes to cut down the salt hay with scythes. They piled great heaps of it in their boats and then poled back to shore, laying it out in the fields above the beaches to cure, to be used in the fall for roof thatching and as winter feed for their animals. Now, year after year, the crops of salt hay grow and die away, unharvested.

Close to the edge of the marsh, a dozen, thirteen, fourteen, great blue herons stand in the tidal flats, still as decoys. They're on their autumn migration and, like us, stay around here just for a few weeks. I almost rouse Marjorie to see them, but then think better of it; let sleeping dogs lie, as they say. She has as little interest in the shorebirds as my grandmother did, who, as my grandfather eagerly pointed them out to her, said only that she found their names hideous—yellowlegs, for goodness sakes (greater and lesser), godwits, black-bellied plovers (which she insisted on calling pot-bellied plovers). Every once in a while one of these enormous, pterodactyl-looking birds takes a cautious step as if walking on a kitchen floor that has just been waxed, suddenly stabbing at the shallows with its dagger bill; a flash of silver, a shake of its head, it gulps its catch and resumes its silent stance.

The Bay opens up for miles behind the marsh, unmarked shoal waters stretching out like some vast unexplored sea. Way back in there, on the outerbeach, that's where Slut's Bush is. In December of 1626, the crew of the forty-foot *Sparrow Hawk,* which was carrying immigrants making their way from England to Virginia, deliberately ran the ship up onto this beach on a calm night. The small ship was out of provisions, there was not enough water for more than a day or two, sickness had broken out among the passengers, and the crew panicked. The next day, some Indian scouts paddled out and spoke to them in English, asking if "they were the Gove'r of Plimoths men, or friends" and offering to bring them to "ye English houses, or carry their letters." When the Indians and two of the *Sparrow Hawk's* crew reached Plymouth, Governor Bradford sent out a rescue party, which arrived several days later. One of the passengers who had been aboard the *Sparrow Hawk,* a Mr. Fells, had brought with him to the New World a woman he described as his maid and housekeeper, but whom the other passengers suspected was his mistress. When it became obvious she was pregnant, the couple was ostracized; and before the rescue party arrived, they were forced to camp out alone on a section of the outerbeach, which forever after has been known as Slut's Bush. Years ago, a storm uncovered the bones of the *Sparrow Hawk* nearby; now they are on display in the museum at Plymouth.

And farther up the outerbeach behind Pochet Island, that's where the *Whydah's* pirates aboard the captured sloop *Mary Anne* were driven ashore in the great storm on the night of April 26, 1717. The next morning, finding themselves safe and rejoicing at their good fortune, they broke out casks of wine, only to be apprehended a few hours later by a justice of the peace and his posse who marched them to Barnstable jail. Later, they were imprisoned in Boston, tried for piracy, and hanged.

And a few miles farther north up the coast was where the pirates' flagship *Whydah* wrecked that same Friday night after a year of piracy on the Spanish Main. Since then, after nor'easters have stirred up surf and sand, sharp-eyed beachcombers have found along the beach the blackened pieces of eight of pirate lore.

The color of the water around the marsh—a Winslow Homer tropic blue where the sun hits the sandy bottom—reveals how far out these shallows extend. I keep the boat in the channel right alongside the edge of the flats, where, off one side, I can see sand riffles an inch or two beneath the surface, with broken conch shells lying here and there, and off the other side, the dark green water where the lobstermen lower their traps into the cold depths.

"Coming about," I say to advise our passenger and crew that we'll be changing tacks.

"Ready about."

No one bothers to move.

"Hard a'lee."

The sail flaps as the breeze slips out. The boom creaks and groans. Then, in slow motion, the sail catches the air again and, with a lurch, billows. I head over toward the mainland, lining up with High Scatteree, the old mansion with the captain's walk atop the bluff at Minister Point, sailing in close to the boats moored off the town landing (more heavy work boats now, I note, than pleasure craft, which, one by one, have been hauled out and put to bed to await another summer), then up the Bay toward the outerbeach.

Distances always feel greater out on the Bay. The outerbeach seems as remote as another continent, with its cluster of tiny, weatherbeaten beach shacks haphazardly nestled in behind the dunes, survivors of decades of hurricanes and winter storms.

Out here, where the painted lobster buoys are

bobbing along the edge of the channel, here on expeditions past we'd head straight in to the outerbeach and sail right up to shore. We'd unload the gear, piling it on the beach, and then wade the boat out to where the water was up to our armpits to anchor so that it wouldn't be left high and dry as the tide turned or if the wind shifted. Then we'd set off along the sandy paths through the rolling waves of beach grass, past clumps of dusty miller with its gray leaves frosted in the summer sun, past the washouts where some winter storm had breached the dunes and littered the sand with driftwood from northern waters. Our feet would sink deep into the hot, soft sand, this, the finest of all sands that, for an eternity, has been washed down the coast from the highland cliffs and dunes, polished by the sea, and sorted and sifted by wind and wave.

Trudging this burning Sahara, we'd hear the hollow booming of the breakers and, over a dune, see the square top of the lookout tower of the abandoned Old Harbor Coast Guard Station and then, finally, cresting a dune, there before us, the Atlantic. Not another soul in sight, just the breaking waves, the white beach curving north and south into infinity, and blue ocean.

The beach never looked the same on successive

visits. Sometimes, though the day was calm, enormous waves would be crashing right up on the shore, and we could see in their marbled green volute as they rose up and, for a moment, hung suspended, schools of fish passing. Other times the waves were breaking out on an offshore bar and then tumbling in over each other like a litter of puppies, running up the beach with a swish before being sucked back down. In the shallows we'd find a treasure trove of sparkling beach pebbles, smoothed to glistening perfection. And once, walking through these shallows, only once, there at last were the sand dollars for which I had searched for years. And once, only once, an inner bar had created behind it up on the beach an Olympic-sized pool, a good five feet deep, its calm, crystal waters as luxurious for a swim as a South Seas lagoon.

On beach blankets on the upper beach, we'd eat our picnic lunch and drink the cold lemonade from the Scotch cooler as the hypnotic spill and crash of the surf sounded in the summer dunes and the summer wind swept through the beach grass. It was easy to understand how Henry Beston, a thirty-nine-year-old schoolteacher, had come to this outerbeach for a two-week vacation in September 1927 to the tiny shack he had built atop a dune, a little north of here, and ended up staying a year. "I lingered on, and as the year lengthened into autumn, the beauty and the mystery of this earth and outer sea so possessed and held me that I could not go." Sitting at his small kitchen table "overlooking the North Atlantic and the dunes, the little room full of the yellow sunlight reflected from the sands and the great sound of the sea," Beston wrote his classic *The Outermost House*, a book which, since publication in 1928, has never been out of print. Here, too, was the beach, a little farther up the coast, that Henry David Thoreau walked in 1849, leaving his Walden Pond "to get a better view than I had yet had of the ocean." The Great Beach, he called it. "What are springs and waterfalls?" he rhapsodized at the end of his account. "Here is the spring of springs, the waterfall of waterfalls. A man may stand there and put all America behind him."

"Someday, Amy," I say, picking her up and setting her on the seat so she can see, "not today, okay? but someday we'll land there so you can walk over and see the ocean."

I picture us walking along the miles of empty beach down on the hard sand just above where the waves were breaking, feeling the warmth of the rising sun, splashing through the ice-cold spill of the breakers.

I don't think Amy pictures that. She takes a quick look to verify that we indeed are in the midst of the Bermuda Triangle, and quickly jumps down to return to the safety of her cabin behind my legs.

Here, where the channel swings in and runs parallel to the outerbeach, here the water under the boat deepens and turns clear green as the sun makes its way down deep to the sandy bottom. We can smell the ocean now, and the channel buoys are larger so that the fishing boats coming in through the inlet in bad weather can spot them. I sail close to one and watch as the ebbing tide pulls at it, the water swirling around its algae-slickened base and chain, trying, with the ferocity of Charybdis, to drag it under.

That's quite a powerful little pull, I think to myself, staring at the eddy that looks like it could suck down the *Queen Mary*. What if, what if when we get nearer to the inlet, the tide is still going out and its pull is stronger than the breeze and I can't stop the boat from being swept out to sea?

Tern Island lies ahead, just off the Cow Yard, a wisp of a sandy islet that used to be the nesting area for hundreds and hundreds of terns. We could land there if we had to. Quite a few years ago, the terns for some reason relocated a mile or two down the

Bay to Monomoy Island, just as the thousands of gulls that once nested on Little Sipson Island—from a distance we could always see a white haze of gulls circling the island and from across the Bay, if we listened, hear their constant calls and cries merge as a raucous noise—have also settled on Monomoy.

I remember that summer morning we walked the shores of Monomoy on the ocean side, pretty much minding our own business, walking right above where the waves were breaking in rhythmic perpetual motion, when a tern spotted us and began its strident, insistent, not-to-be-ignored shrieking. Quickly it was jointed by a comrade and then another, hovering in tight formation above us.

And then their air raids began. Climbing twenty feet, they plummeted in a free fall, no, faster than a free fall, a real dive bombing maneuver with their orange bayonet beaks pointed straight at us, leveling off not more than ten inches above our prickling scalps. One after the other they dove, climbed up and dove again, with no letup. We took off down the beach at a run, three adults pursued by these pint-sized fighter pilots in crisp white uniforms and black helmets, spitting bursts of scolding screeches. These terns, descendants of the ones that Henry Thoreau noted on his walk along the outerbeach in 1849 would "pursue the traveller anxiously, now and then diving close to his head with a squeak" and that in 1928 chased Henry Beston "all the way to Nauset," chased us a good quarter mile down the beach before flying back to their base.

We glide by Tern Island and then the fish pier with its gulls lined up on the rail of the observation deck waiting patiently for a late afternoon buffet when the boats return from the sea and the fishermen pitchfork their catch from the holds onto the conveyor belts. Beyond the fish pier, beyond the Chatham Bars Inn, the swells coming in through the inlet begin ever so gently to rock us. Ahead, the open water is moving with rips and currents; and farther out, off the tip of the outerbeach at the inlet, surf explodes into spray and seething white water foams over the bars.

From the days of the Pilgrims, whose *Mayflower* almost foundered right here off the outerbeach, over three thousand ships have wrecked on this lonely forty-mile stretch of outer coast. Barks. Brigs. Schooners. Sloops. Steamers. Freighters. Tragedy after tragedy. "The annals of this voracious beach!" Thoreau exclaimed on his trip to the Cape.

> Who would write them, unless it were a ship-
> wrecked sailor? How many have seen it only
> in the midst of danger and distress, the last

strip of earth which their mortal eyes behold. Think of the amount of suffering which a single strand has witnessed! The ancients would have represented it as a sea monster with open jaws, more terrible than Scylla and Charybdis.

It was as horrifying as if today, plane after plane crashed at one particular airport. "What tales about warm stoves," Henry Beston wrote, moved by the Elizabethan drama of it all, "wreckage coming ashore, voices and cries in the wild dark, and no ship to be seen, ships in a bitter northeast gale with sails frozen hard as boards and the dead men in the rigging mummies of ice, the terrible wreck of the *Castagna*, the death of the crew, and the shivering, half-alive canary found next morning in the soppy cabin."

I shiver and come about to head back to quieter waters, back toward home. And with the wind freshening just a bit, we skim past the sandy beach of the Inn, past the fish pier with its observant gulls, past Tern Island, in toward the headland of Minster Point.

Contrary to my sister's and certainly Amy's misgivings, this maiden voyage has been carefully plotted and planned so that the tide, now coming in, helps carry us smartly along. Yes, with the foresight of a Magellan, a Frobisher, a Drake, a . . .

"Damn!"

Uh, oh. Big mistake. Rule Number One of skippering is that the captain should never swear aloud while at the helm. Perhaps a "No problem, ma'm, we just grazed the side of that darn iceberg," or a "Wait till you see our watertight compartments in operation!" or a "It's just a short distance from here to Halifax," but never a curse, unless it's "shiver me timbers."

"What happened?" Marjorie demands, instantly wide awake.

And by the terrified look in her eyes, I know Amy is saying to herself, *I knew this was going to happen. I knew this was going to happen.*

"Nothing," I say. "No problem."

"We're not even moving. What the hell did you do?"

"No, it just got a little too shallow here."

"Oh, great. So now what? Are we stuck?"

"No. Here. I'll just raise the centerboard," I say casually, struggling with all my might to raise the damn thing without popping beads of sweat.

No go. "Hmmmmmm."'

"What? Is this thing stuck here? I'm not sitting out here all day waiting for the tide to come in."

"No, No. We don't have to," I say reassuringly, ready to maroon my scurvy crew on the nearest excuse for an island. "We just have to get out and give it a push."

"No way. I'm not getting out here," my sister declares as if I had suggested she carry the boat home on her shoulders. "You're crazy if you think I'm getting out," she adds, peering suspiciously over the side at the eelgrass-covered flat, which, I admit, is a tad sinister looking. One wouldn't have too clear of an idea on what, or on whom, one was setting one's feet.

"Come on. We have to get the weight out of the boat to float it."

"No way. I told you, I'm not getting out in that crap. You got us into this." And back she leans against her life cushion and closes her eyes.

Amy looks over the side with an equally jaundiced eye. I'm not about to ask her to get out because she's just waiting for the least little excuse to abandon ship and take her chances out in the shipping lanes.

"Don't panic, Amy," I say, keeping up a cheerful monologue to buoy her spirits as I go over the side, easing gingerly into the soft ooze and trying not to grimace as it squishes up between my toes; it feels like I've stepped right onto the slippery bellies of a congregation of eels.

Amy is decidedly concerned. The fact that I'm rocking the boat back and forth trying to break the ooze's hold probably isn't reassuring her.

"Under the circumstances, Amy," Marjorie notes for the official log of this voyage, "mutiny, you know, is entirely justified. Our stupid captain has taken us who knows where. We're lost. We're sinking. Will we ever reach port again? I, for one, doubt it. What, oh what, shall we do? What did you say, Amy? A mutiny? Yes! But is that not unlawful? Remember Fletcher Christian. Right you are. Under the circumstances it is justified. Let's throw him in the irons."

With a satisfying slurp, the boat breaks free of the muck. Step by cautious step, I manhandle it out toward deeper water.

"I think I'd rather take my chances being marooned on that lonely atoll," I say, pointing back toward Tern Island. "Your first mate looks armed to the teeth."

The boat is floating; the channel is nearby.

The fair breeze carries us back around Minister Point and down the Bay, all the way past Fox Hill. Amy is up on the seat now, looking toward home, greedily smelling the familiar scents of home territory.

"Where are you going?" Marjorie asks.

"In."

"In? Is this all? Let's at least go as far as the yacht club."

Ah, this is a change. Could it be that my sister is actually enjoying our morning sail? I will test my theory.

"I think Amy's had enough," I suggest.

"Amy hasn't had enough. And don't always blame everything on Amy just because you don't want to do it."

Amy is looking longingly at her beach and her home. By now she's convinced she's aboard the *Mary Celeste*, the mystery ship that put to sea, its crew never to be seen again.

"This is as far as we're going?" Marjorie persists. "Well, this wasn't worth it at all. Let's at least go to the town landing dock. I'm telling your parents you wouldn't take us for a decent sail."

A sailboat moves along the far west shore, up toward the Narrows. It's the only other boat we've seen out on the Bay this morning. We know what that means. The summer sailing camps closed a few weeks ago. The schoolchildren and college students have gone. We too, are not exempt from such annual migratory flights and will be leaving in a few days, on Labor Day. "There is no word in the language for end-of-summer sadness," E. B. White once wrote, "but the human spirit has a word for it and picks up the first sound of its approach." We see its approach in the slant of sunlight—the sun's farther west than it should be right before noon; in the autumnal blue of the Bay; the new shape of clouds; in the clarity of the sky—no summer heat haze today. We feel its approach in the coolness of the bright noon hour. We smell its approach in the breeze, carrying the aroma of the goldening marshes. We hear it in the drone of the cricket chorus from the salt meadows: *six weeks till frost, six weeks till frost*. Evenings lengthen and the golden days grow shorter. Suddenly, each day becomes precious, something to be hoarded like candy in a child's pocket. We savor the warmth of the hour. A little longer sail, yes.

Observing us heading in the wrong direction—away from the dinghy—Amy appears to be counting her beads, though her trembling has subsided. She's gotten to the point where she is ready to accept her fate. Maybe just a little more won't do any lasting harm.

"Okay, but that's as far as we're going 'cause it'll

be too hard to come back against the tide."

"Jeez! Can't this boat do anything? I knew they should've gotten a better boat."

With that, she settles back again against the life cushion, now looking all around, enjoying the morning.

Down the Pilgrims' route toward the town landing and a little beyond for good measure, and then, with the morning breeze, we tack back against the tide. With the entire crew now enthusiastically assisting—Amy is up at the bow pointing the way home to make sure we don't miss it this time, and Marjorie is manning the boat hook to catch the mooring can as we approach — we make a smart landing on the first pass and are back to port in time for lunch.

On the beach, Amy shakes and shakes again as if to wake from a bad dream and convince herself that none of this really, truly happened, rolls on her back in the sand in blessed happiness (probably the dog-world equivalent of kissing the ground and pledging never to leave terra firma again) and dashes joyfully up the path to the house ahead of Marjorie. And I, like one of the Volga boatmen, struggle to haul the dinghy out of the water up through the sand, grunting and groaning, an inch gained, two, three, yoo heave ho! yoo heave ho! to its place in the beach grass above the high-tide line. When the spots swimming in front of my eyes begin to subside, I gather up the oars, the life cushions, the canvas bag, and the paddle and, barely balancing the load, make my way up the path.

"He got it stuck on some stupid sandbar," I hear Marjorie telling our parents as I stumble onto the lawn.

And not a word of dissent do I hear from Amy who seems to be solemnly nodding her head in agreement.

Golden retrievers are water dogs; and I could see us, in summers future, sailing the Bay, Amy sitting at attention in the bow, scouting the shore, the islands, assuming the role of commanding officer whose duty it was to pilot the ship to port, a determined look in her eyes like you see in old nineteenth-century portraits of sea captains. I could picture us on a lazy September afternoon sailing up the twisting estuary that leads to Meeting House Pond, the sky and the Bay that beautiful deep blue of Indian summer, the salt meadows turning gold. On an August flood tide, we would take the boat into the tidal creeks that split off again and again, making a maze in the Strong Island marsh, where, in the fall, the hunters would be waiting in the duck blinds; that was great retriever territory and I could see Amy looking, figuring out just what went on in there. And, of course, there would be the races, where Amy, her ears blowing back in the breeze, would growl menacingly at any boat that tried to slip ahead of us.

That was my picture. Amy's remained quite different.

If Amy viewed us, parading single file from the house to the beach for a swim in the Bay as lemmings marching to sea, to her our boating expeditions remained nothing short of demented kamikaze missions. I wouldn't have been surprised at all if she named our dinghy whatever the equivalent in dog language would be for the *Andrea Doria* and our sailboat the *Titanic*. She avoided them both at all costs.

Once, when we tied up at the mooring at the end of a day's sail, one of our sharp-eyed sailors happened to glance up at the house and spot in the upstairs window: a retriever face.

Amy had climbed the stairs to the second floor and there had jumped up onto the loveseat by the window to get the best view of us, just like a captain's wife climbing to the widow's walk atop her New England house with telescope in hand to scan the seas for the return of her husband. There, on the loveseat, she paced anxiously, watching, worrying, awaiting our return. And when at last we walked up the bluff, there was, of course, her jig of joy, and her unspoken admonition, the exact same as that of the pirates who once sailed the Caribbean: "If Tortuga let you pass, you beware of Hatteras." Which, translated into golden retriever language, probably is something like *You were lucky that time, pack members; don't ever be so dimwitted again!*

Chapter Seven

Partings

"Time to get ready," my father announces at 4:45, knowing it will take us at least a good hour to get the sand and saltwater and suntan lotion off and make ourselves reasonably presentable to go out for dinner.

Amy immediately notes a change in tempo of the household routine, a new sense of direction as we drop what we're doing and go to our rooms to get cleaned up and changed.

As I turn off the water in the bathroom, I brace for what I expect to hear: a paw scratching at the door.

There it is. Oh boy, here we go.

I open the door and there stands Amy, tennis ball in mouth, body twitching with excitement, her expression shouting, *Me too! me too!*

A pang of guilt. This is going to take some explaining. "Amy? Amy? Okay, I've got to tell you what we're doing."

She swings her head back to get a better grip on the ball, crouches down on her front paws, then springs back to a full alert standing position, trying to get me moving faster toward this new hunt.

"Amy?" I get down on my knees in front of her, smooth down her velvet ears, and quietly explain just what is happening.

"Amy, we have to go out for dinner, okay?"

For a split second, she looks like she understands exactly what I'm saying and all its implications, but then catches herself, not ready to give up so easily. Out of the corner of her eye, she spots a glimpse of sock, loose on the floor, slyly looks back at me, and then edges toward it.

I grab the sock and put it on the bureau.

She drops her tennis ball and stares up at it, contemplating her next move.

"Okay, now listen," I start again. "We have to go out to dinner, okay?"

She stops looking at the sock. She looks at me, her expression beginning to change from anticipation of a new adventure to bad news a'coming.

"Okay, see, we have to go out to dinner, but we'll be right back. Okay? We'll be right back."

Oh, is she good! Sir Laurence Olivier? Helen Hayes? Rank theatrical amateurs in comparison with golden retrievers. Within a second, without missing a beat or changing costumes or makeup, she has gone from joyous anticipation to a new widow's deep despondency.

"Okay, Amy?" I pat her, tickling under her ears where she likes it. "It'll just be for a little bit. And you know their rule about no dogs in the dining room. I know, I don't know why they have that rule. No, you don't slobber. Yes, you're a very, very neat eater. But listen. We'll be right back, okay?"

She refuses to look at me as I pat her, turning her head to the side, and in the middle of my mumbling inept apologies, quietly turns and, as if to a dirge, walks out. Across the kitchen floor I hear her toenails clicking.

I know exactly where she's gone. And when finally we're ready and gather in the front hall to leave, there she is, sitting in the living room next to the picture window, not looking out at the sun on the Bay or at the two rabbits playing tag on the lawn or at the covey of quail emerging from the bayberry bushes to search for their dinner of grubs in the grass. Oh, no: she's sitting there staring straight at the back of the big old arm chair by the window.

Clearly we've done wrong. We have broken a

fundamental covenant of her pack: that we all are the same—fellow rovers on earth for a moment in time— one for all and all for one; a covenant of eternal friendship. We are leaving her. Like sinners, one by one we slink to the front door, ashamed of ourselves.

"We'll be right back, okay?"

"Amy, be good. You watch the house."

"Hurry up! hurry up!" my father orders.

Not even a glance. She looks at none of us, keeping her eyes straight ahead, staring sadly at the middle of the back of the big old chair.

Feeling like we have betrayed our best friend and not that interested after all in going out ("Should we save the money and stay home and finish the meatloaf?" "It's too late now, we have reservations." "Don't be ridiculous, she'll be fine."), we sneak out the front door, quietly closing it behind us.

From our table by the floor-to-ceiling windows, we watch the sun setting behind the pine-covered hills across the Bay as a lone sailboat makes its way back to harbor. The shallow bowl of New England clam chowder with oyster crackers floating in it is the taste of summer, the last drops of it mopped up with a piece of one of those little homemade muffins, moist with native blueberries. Swordfish, caught offshore that day, and then the warm Indian pudding, as it can be made only on Cape Cod, with just a dollop of vanilla ice cream on top. Oh, yes! But in the back of all our minds is our friend, home alone, staring at the back of a chair, waiting for our return.

Our nagging concern, of course, is that maybe it isn't acting, that maybe golden retrievers experience a range of emotions unknown to humans, higher highs and lower lows, uncontrollable joy we can only dream of, unthinkable loneliness and despair we can only hope we'll never confront. Mixed together in our huckleberry friend is a child's exuberance, a sense of wonder of the moment, and a philosopher's perception of "time's winged chariot hurrying near." *Why, when our time is so short,* she seems to question at each departure, *why would you even think of leaving?*

So, as much as we want to linger to look at the perennial garden to try to figure out just how they get it looking so good with the regal delphiniums blue as the Bay, mounds of coreopsis shining like tiny suns, shasta daisies that whisper of summer meadows, and the purple lavender, scenting the darkening September evening, we hurry along to the car and home.

Golden retrievers know how to make you feel lower than a flea on a cat's belly, but they never, ever hold a grudge.

We open the front door. There she is, quivering with delight, squealing her joyous welcome, racing from one to another, jumping up and hugging the legs of those whose legs need hugging, wriggling from head to tail in pure happiness, squeaking in excitement, making it quite clear that all is forgiven. From bottomless dejection to boundless joy. Her family is home. Her pack is back. One. Two. Three. Four. All here. All's right with the world. Who could ask for anything more?

The worst, of course, is at the end of a ten-day or two-week stay. By then, Amy has convinced herself, quite logically, that we have come to our senses and agreed forevermore to be a part of her pack. So sure of it is she that she has begun to cut down the number of her nightly bed checks to confirm we are still there. Of course we're still there. We will always be there.

And then early one morning, a morning just like every other morning, a morning when our first weather observation notes the sun rising above the Strong Island marsh and sparkling on the blue water of the channel, a day with a brisk sailing breeze blowing through the apple tree outside the dining room window, a day that will be perfect for another adventure, there, on such a morning, suddenly out of nowhere, there by the front door is: a suitcase. Once Amy catches sight of it and stares for a moment at it, it's as if the light were leaving her life, forever. No interest in eating. No interest in what is going on at the breakfast table. No interest even in a nibble of banana. *It's happening again, damn it all,* she says to herself, or retriever words to that effect. *They're deserting my pack again.*

"You're in complete charge, you know," my sister instructs me if she's the one who has to leave a few days before me. "Take her to Morris Island right after breakfast, okay?"

"Yeah, we will."

"And plenty of dog work."

"We will."

"Otherwise, she's going to be morose."

"I know."

"You're in charge."

"I know," I say, knowing full well the questioning looks I will get that day, and the way, halfway down the beach at Morris Island on a beautiful morning, Amy will remember, and stop, and refuse to take another step forward, and how, when she gets me walking in the right direction—back to the car—she will pick up speed and fast walk all the way to the road, looking neither to the right nor to the left, and wait by the door of the car to get in, and, when we get home, the vigils by the front door, and the wandering into the empty bedroom during the day, and the bed checks for the next few nights that, night after night, reveal an empty bed, and the toenails clicking across the kitchen floor on her way back to her bed.

Chapter Eight

October Light

And that was it. That was how it was that Saturday morning lying next to Amy in the front hall in a pool of October sunlight when Death pulled at our ears and whispered in the stir of oak leaves out on the lawn, "Live! I'm coming." Moments of life are what we remembered.

How good it felt to be curled up safe and warm inside with a nor'easter roaring through the pines and rattling the window casings and the rain driving against the side of the house.

The exuberance of a homecoming welcome.

Shadows of clouds racing across the lawn on a windy day.

Clear, silent nights when the Milky Way bridged sea and sky, and faraway, the breakers booming along the outerbeach.

The summer smell of the salt marsh in late afternoon.

Walking through sand, scuffling through pine needles.

The call of a mourning dove on a fog-bound morning.

Sharing a container of lemon yogurt.

Waking in the middle of the night to see Amy staring, her head resting on the mattress next to the pillow, the thumping of her tail against the bed when she saw you open an eye.

How every day, anything and everything could be wondrous.

"Good times, Amy. We had good times, didn't we?" She looked at me now with a look I had seen before, that something's-wrong-something-isn't-right-please-help-me look.

Every other time we'd known what to do.

On winter walks through the snow, sometimes she'd stop short and sit down, refusing to take another step. We'd check her paws and sure enough, there between the pads were hard little ice pellets, which we plopped out, one by one, and off we'd go. The big, ugly, hateful ticks, swollen and bloated with her blood, we'd pick off and drop into the tin can filled with Whisk, and untangle the prickly twigs caught in her coat that she couldn't chew out, and snip off the hair mats from behind her ears and show them to her, and scratch the places she showed us that needed scratching and always have a bowl of cool water ready when she was thirsty. Here were people who could be pretty handy pack members, sometimes, who give delicious tomato juice baths to those squirted with stinky skunk juice, who drive cars faster than any animal can run, who go out on hunts and, without breaking a sweat, return home with bag after bag of prey to be stored in the kitchen, who open doors and make a room light or dark. *Oh ye gods who walk the earth and routinely work miracles,* I read in her big brown eyes looking, looking into mine, *help me now.*

Yet now for her, for her who for ten years, day and night, had watched so steadfastly over us like the most devoted, adoring nanny, for her now, when she needed us, we could do nothing.

She closed her eyes and was dozing, breathing shallowly.

It was time to go. It was time to say good-bye.

"Amy? I have to go, okay? I have to go. You be all right, okay?"

I was whispering into her fur so she wouldn't hear me crying.

"Amy, okay, look"—here was something good—"tomorrow: tomorrow morning, okay? Amy. Jean. And Bill. Go to Cape Cod. Tomorrow!"

She was listening.

"Tomorrow morning: Amy, Jean, and Bill, go to Cape Cod, okay Amy? Amy'll be better there."

My face was buried in her shoulder in the warm wonderful fresh smell of her that I wanted always to remember.

"Okay, Amy? Whatever happens, we'll all be together, right?" Was that right? Was it possible? "And Scotch."

Her ears twitched, and I was pretty sure she remembered Scotch, her favorite golden retriever friend in New Jersey who had been hit by the UPS truck two years ago.

"And Brambles, too, okay?"

Brambles she definitely remembered, her Cape Cod retriever sidekick who had died last year.

Squeezing my eyes shut against her, I prayed they really would be. Please, whatever happens, don't let her suffer.

The morning breeze stirred the brown oak leaves on the lawn and blew through the screen. Her nose twitched, breathing the autumn green grass, dying leaves smell.

"How did we do, Amy? How did we do? Was it okay, living with us? Was it a good life for a retriever?"

I hoped it had been.

"Was it as good for you as it was for us? Were we okay as members of your pack?"

She had taken us places we never would have gone and shown us things we never would have seen without her. Had we understood everything she showed us? Everything about fairness and faithfulness, about unconditional friendship and loyalty and love?

"Exult," she had taught us. "Now, right now, is a miracle. Every day, an adventure!" "Sing praise," had been her message. "Bark and shout with joy! We are alive in the wonder of today. Drink in the love of life, the love of love."

There has always been something extraordinary going on between humans and dogs during the twenty thousand years they have chosen to live together and had a mutual admiration society. What was this enduring emotional bond between people and their evolutionary cousins?

The ancients believed they would find dogs in Heaven.

And when Alexander the Great's dog, Peritas,

died at the age of eleven, the conqueror named a city after him.

And it was "patient-hearted Odysseus' dog," Argos, who was the only one to recognize Odysseus when he returned home after his years of war and wanderings, who "wagged his tail, and laid both his ears back; only he now no longer had the strength to move any closer to his master."

And the Roman poet Martial wrote that Publius' dog, Issa, was "worth all the costly pearls of India; sorrow and joy she feels as much as he does."

And Lord Byron in 1808 inscribed a monument for his Newfoundland dog, Boatswain (in whose tomb he reserved a place for himself):

> Near this spot are deposited the remains of one who possessed Beauty without Vanity, Strength without Insolence, Courage without Ferocity, and all the Virtues of Man, without his Vices. This Praise, which would be unmeaning Flattery if inscribed over human ashes, is but a just tribute to the Memory of Boatswain, a Dog.

"How was it, Amy? Me? I wouldn't have changed a minute."

I patted her and smoothed her coat, now white in

more spots than golden.

"Bye, bye, Amy, okay?"

I stood up and walked to the front door and looked at her lying there, her eyes not moving from mine.

Long last looks.

I walked back to her and kissed her head.

"Bye, bye, Amy. You be good girl, okay? Bye, bye, Amy. I love you."

The smallest flip of the tip of her tail. Tired, very tired, she was asleep again, dreaming, I'm sure, of the kind of morning when the northwest wind blows down the Bay from the islands.

And all I ask is a merry yarn from a laughing
　　fellow-rover,
And quiet sleep and a sweet dream when the
　　long trick's over.

I quietly shut the front door.

Early the next morning I drove to my parents' house, wondering if I might be able to help, worried I might get in the way, afraid of what I would find. How could they even get Amy outside and into the car? But the shades were drawn, the house quiet. They already were gone.

"No problem," they reported that afternoon

when they called from the Cape. "Amy went out the front door and walked down the driveway as good as can be, no limp, and jumped, like a circus dog, right into the back seat, and slept all the way up."

Way to go, Amy. What a dog.

When they pulled into their driveway at the Cape and Amy realized where she was, she had perked up and walked down the path to the beach to explore. ("Live," Death whispered in the wind through the beach grass; "I'm coming.")

"So we'll just have to watch her and take one day at a time. We'll make an appointment tomorrow at the vet's to have her blood checked again and see what he thinks."

But that was the last good news.

When the veterinarian compared the blood test and x-rays he took with the ones from New Jersey a few days before, he could see that the lymphatic cancer had spread.

And when I called the next evening, she was gone.

Wrestling with the infinite, the inexplicable, the unjustifiable, maybe we look for signs or maybe we're just more receptive to them. Several mornings later, a noise outside my third-floor office window caught my attention, and then, there it was: a crow had flown by the window so close that either it touched the glass or I could hear through the window the beating of its wings. A few seconds later, it flew back by my window and alighted there on top of a birch tree. Sitting atop the birch, not twelve feet from my window, it stared straight at me and cawed, sounding just like a dog. Down past my window again it swooped, returning to the birch tree and cawing again. Three times it repeated its jest and then flew off. And I was sure, on that lonely fall morning, I was sure it was bringing a message that everything was alright. *Don't forget me*, the crow had cawed. *Don't forget me*. And it was then I knew that Amy would stay with us.

Does that seem so strange? Does it seem so impossible that Amy, who had looked out for us for so long, would have tried to move heaven and earth to let us know somehow she was okay? Does a lifetime of love vanish just like that? Poof! Gone? I doubted it.

For a while, she was everywhere.

In the rustle of the dry oak leaves out on the driveway.

In the sigh of the wind through the hemlocks on the side of the house and the way their swaying made the sunlight and shadows swim on the floor of the sunroom where she would have been lying, listening.

In her favorite places around my parents' house, so

that when I went over to check on the house it didn't seem right to put away her toys: the rubber football and green frog she had left in the corner of the den, the rawhide bone by her bed that she hadn't finished chewing, the tennis balls she had so carefully hidden around the house.

She was everywhere then, and it didn't seem such a great distance at all between where I was and where she was. It seemed that if I just called for her loud enough, wherever she was, she would hear.

And there are times, even now, when a sound, a flicker of motion, will catch my attention; and looking up from what I'm doing and out the window of wherever I am, I sort of expect that I might see her, I half think that there she will be, out across the lawn, sniffing under the pines to pick up a scent, looking for something. And I'd try to catch her one last time. I would smash past anyone who was in my way. I would take a chair and break out the window if I had to and run to her. She'd look up and see me and race toward me, making her retriever noises of happiness, her tail going in circles, and I'd be running toward her and we'd tackle each other and roll in the grass, and I'd hold her, forever.

But now rest, tender shepherd. Your work is done. Your pack safe. Thank you for watching over us.

erudite vocab

Cashun
Xmas
Burton is to
    play

Side Marjorie
    Army

Piggy

Changing shoe line